RELIGION AND THE LAW

by

Margaret C. Jasper, Esq.

Oceana's Legal Almanac Series:
Law for the Layperson

1998
Oceana Publications, Inc.
Dobbs Ferry, N.Y.

Information contained in this work has been obtained by Oceana Publications from sources believed to be reliable. However, neither the Publisher nor its authors guarantee the accuracy or completeness of any information published herein, and neither Oceana nor its authors shall be responsible for any errors, omissions or damages arising from the use of this information. This work is published with the understanding that Oceana and its authors are supplying information, but are not attempting to render legal or other professional services. If such services are required, the assistance of an appropriate professional should be sought.

You may order this or any other Oceana publications by visiting Oceana's Web Site at http://www.oceanalaw.com

---

Library of Congress Cataloging-in-Publication Data

Jasper, Margaret C.
   Religion and the law / by Margaret C. Jasper.
      p. cm.—(Oceana's legal almanac series. Law for the layperson)
   Includes bibliographical references.
   ISBN 0-379-11327-9 (acid-free paper)
   1. Religion and law—United States—Popular works.
   2. Church and state—United States—Popular works.
   3. Freedom of religion—United States—Popular works.
   I. Title. II. Series.
KF4865.Z9J37 1998   98-43941
344.73'096—dc21   CIP

Oceana's Legal Almanac Series: Law for the Layperson
ISSN: 1075-7376

©1998 by Oceana Publications, Inc.

All rights reserved. No part of this publication may be reproduced or transmitted in any form or by any means, electronic or mechanical, including photocopy, recording, xerography, or any information storage and retrieval system, without permission in writing from the publisher.

Manufactured in the United States of America on acid-free paper.

To My Husband Chris

**Your love and support
are my motivation and inspiration**

-and-

In memory of my son, Jimmy

ABOUT THE AUTHOR

MARGARET C. JASPER is an attorney engaged in the general practice of law in South Salem, New York, concentrating in the areas of personal injury and entertainment law. Ms. Jasper holds a Juris Doctor degree from Pace University School of Law, White Plains, New York, is a member of the New York and Connecticut bars, and is certified to practice before the United States District Courts for the Southern and Eastern Districts of New York, and the United States Supreme Court.

Ms. Jasper has been appointed to the panel of arbitrators of the American Arbitration Association and the law guardian panel for the Family Court of the State of New York, is a member of the Association of Trial Lawyers of America, and is a New York State licensed real estate broker and member of the Westchester County Board of Realtors, operating as Jasper Real Estate, in South Salem, New York.

Ms. Jasper is the author and general editor of the following legal almanacs: Juvenile Justice and Children's Law; Marriage and Divorce; Estate Planning; The Law of Contracts; The Law of Dispute Resolution; Law for the Small Business Owner; The Law of Personal Injury; Real Estate Law for the Homeowner and Broker; Everyday Legal Forms; Dictionary of Selected Legal Terms; The Law of Medical Malpractice; The Law of Product Liability; The Law of No-Fault Insurance; The Law of Immigration; The Law of Libel and Slander; The Law of Buying and Selling; Elder Law; The Right to Die; AIDS Law; The Law of Obscenity and Pornography; The Law of Child Custody; The Law of Debt Collection; Consumer Rights Law; Bankruptcy Law for the Individual Debtor; Victim's Rights Law; Animal Rights Law; Workers' Compensation Law; Employee Rights in theWorkplace; Probate Law; Environmental Law; Labor Law; The Americans with Disabilities Act; The Law of Capital Punishment; Education Law; The Law of Violence Against Women; Landlord-Tenant Law; and Insurance Law.

TABLE OF CONTENTS

INTRODUCTION xi
CHAPTER 1: AN OVERVIEW OF THE FIRST
   AMENDMENT AND RELIGIOUS FREEDOM 1
  Historical Background 1
    The Puritans 1
  Article VI of the U.S. Constitution 2
  The Bill of Rights 2
  The First Amendment 3
  Religion and Politics 4
CHAPTER 2: THE ROLE OF THE SUPREME COURT 5
  In General 5
  The Establishment Clause 5
    The Lemon Test 6
  The Free Exercise Clause 6
    The Mormon Cases 7
    The Jehovah's Witnesses Cases 7
  Government Neutrality in Religious Disputes 8
  Financial Assistance to Religious Institutions 9
  The Religious Freedom Restoration Act (RFRA) 9
    The City of Boerne 10
CHAPTER 3: RELIGION IN THE WORKPLACE 13
    Overview 13
  Title VII of the Civil Rights Act of 1964 13
  State Employment Discrimination Statutes 14
  The Role of Religion in the Federal Workplace 14
    Scope of Coverage 14
    Personal Religious Expression 15
    Employment Discrimination 15
    Accommodation of Religious Practices 15
CHAPTER 4: RELIGION IN PUBLIC EDUCATION 17
  In General 17
  Religious Expression 17
  School Prayer 17
  Graduation Prayers 18
  Student Religious Clubs 18

School Curriculum 18
Creationism 19
Religious Apparel 19
School Holidays 19
Baccalaureate Ceremonies 20
Distribution of Religious Literature 20
Released Time 20
The Role of the School District 20
Public Support of Private Schools 20
Statement of First Principles 23
    Sponsors 24
The Equal Access Act 27
    Basic Concepts 27
        Nondiscrimination 27
        Protection 28
        Local Control 28
    Noncurriculum-Related Student Groups 28
CHAPTER 5: NATIVE AMERICAN RELIGIOUS RIGHTS 31
Historical Background 31
The American Indian Religious Freedom Act of 1978 (AIRFA) . . 31
The American Indian Religious Freedom Act Amendments of
1994 31
Presidential Directive on Eagle Feather Distribution 32
Native American Prisoners 32
CHAPTER 6: THE WILLIAMSBURG CHARTER 35
CHAPTER 7: MISCELLANEOUS ISSUES 37
Religion and Child Custody Issues 37
Religion and Prisoners' Rights 37
Religion and Medical Issues 38
Priest-Penitent Privilege 39
APPENDICES 41
  APPENDIX 1 - Directory of Religious Freedom Organizations . . 43
  APPENDIX 2 - Chart of Significant Supreme Court Decisions
    Involving Religion and Public Education 45
  APPENDIX 3 - The Religious Freedom Restoration Act of
    1993 51

TABLE OF CONTENTS

APPENDIX 4 - Federal Guidelines on Religious Exercise
and Expression in the Federal Workplace 55
APPENDIX 5 - Presidential Directive on Religious
Expression in Public Schools, July 13, 1995 67
APPENDIX 6 - Sample School District Policy on Religious
Issues 73
APPENDIX 7 - Statement of First Principles 77
APPENDIX 8 - Directory of Sponsors of the Statement of
First Principles 79
APPENDIX 9 - The Equal Access Act of 1984 83
APPENDIX 10 - American Indian Religious Freedom Act of
1978 (AIRFA) 87
APPENDIX 11 - American Indian Religious Freedom Act
Amendments of 1994 89
APPENDIX 12 - The Williamsburg Charter 93
GLOSSARY 111
BIBLIOGRAPHY 115

INTRODUCTION

The United States is the most religiously diverse country in the world. For the most part, Americans have learned to live together and respect the differences which exist among the various religious denominations. This is quite remarkable given the overwhelming number of "holy wars" that have endured throughout the world during the twentieth century.

The framers of the United States Constitution recognized that religious freedom cannot succeed when a governing body interferes in, or exercises control over, religious matters. Thus, the Constitution grants its citizens unprecedented religious liberty under the First Amendment. The unparalleled diversity of religion in the United States is due almost entirely to this full protection of religious freedom guaranteed by the Constitution.

This legal almanac explores the law of religion in America, including its early history, evolvement, and current status, and examines legislative efforts to clarify and reaffirm the liberties and prohibitions guaranteed by the First Amendment in religious matters. It further sets forth the role the Supreme Court has taken in interpreting and protecting the principles embraced by the Constitution, and explores the appropriate role of religion in such areas as education, employment, and child custody. In addition, the religious issues facing Native Americans, and the rights they have gained over the last two decades, are also discussed.

The Appendix provides resource directories, relevant statutes, sample documents; and other pertinent information and data. The Glossary contains definitions of many of the terms used throughout the almanac.

CHAPTER 1:

AN OVERVIEW OF THE FIRST AMENDMENT AND RELIGIOUS FREEDOM

Historical Background

In the early 1600's, many people left their native countries seeking refuge in the "New World" from religious persecution. This shared experience of religious intolerance caused the nation's founders to make religious freedom a priority, limiting government's involvement in religious matters. They did not want to completely exclude religion from American life, as it was an important factor in the day-to-day life of the early settlers. However, they did want to ensure that religious liberty—the right to freely practice the religion of one's choice—was never again controlled by an oppressive, intolerant government.

Most of the European settlers who arrived in America came from countries that had well-established churches—e.g., England, Spain and France—and the Church was central to all aspects of community and political life. The separation of religion and government in America, and the freedoms guaranteed all religious groups, was an unprecedented experiment.

The Puritans

The Puritans were a group of people who fled England due to religious persecution. They came to America seeking religious freedom, and established the Massachusetts colony. The Puritans believed that they were called by God to establish a commonwealth based on a covenant between God and themselves as God's people. All laws of the colony were to be grounded in God's law, and all citizens were expected to uphold this divine covenant.

The Puritan concept was challenged by Roger Williams, a Puritan minister, who expressed a different view of God's plan. Williams believed in separation of church and state, and disagreed with the concept that God had given divine sanction to the Puritans. He argued that the true church was a voluntary association of God's elect, and warned that coercion in religious matters has historically led to intolerance and persecution. He further proposed that state involvement in religion was actually contrary to God's divine will because every individual was free to accept or reject God's word—a concept known as "Freedom of Conscience."

Williams was subsequently banished from Massachusetts due to his beliefs. Thereafter, he founded Rhode Island as a colony where all religious groups were welcome. Gradually, this extension of religious liberty to all religious groups became the principal American view, and the forerunner of the First Amendment to the U.S. Constitution which followed approximately 150 years later.

Since that time, the United States has expanded far beyond the largely Protestant pluralism of its early history, embracing approximately 3000 religious groups, as well as those who express no religious beliefs whatsoever.

Article VI of the U.S. Constitution

The only mention of religion in the Constitution of the United States prior to the adoption of the First Amendment was the "no religious test" provision of Article VI, which states: "[N]o religious test shall ever be required as a qualification to any office or public trust under the United States."

At the time of the Constitutional Convention in 1787, most of the colonies still conducted religious tests for office. The "no religious test" provision passed with little dissent, formally abolishing one of the most powerful tools a state had to oppress religious diversion. This was a significant step in the development of religious liberty in America.

Thereafter, most states abolished their own religious tests for state office. Thus, it is unconstitutional for any state to require an officeholder to declare a belief in God as a requirement for taking office at any level of government.

The Bill of Rights

James Madison and other members of the Constitutional Convention believed that the Constitution established a limited federal government with no control over religious matters. However, many Americans, including religious leaders, were concerned that the Constitution offered inadequate protection of their civil and religious rights. Therefore, as a compromise, Madison agreed to propose a Bill of Rights to satisfy any adversaries who might delay adoption of the Constitution.

Madison's original proposal for a Bill of Rights provision concerning religion stated:

> "The civil rights of none shall be abridged on account of religious belief or worship, nor shall any national religion be established, nor shall the full and equal rights of conscience be in any manner, or on any pretence, infringed."

This language was altered in the House to read:

"Congress shall make no law establishing religion, or to prevent the free exercise thereof, or to infringe the rights of conscience."

The Senate's proposed clause read:

"Congress shall make no law establishing articles of faith, or a mode of worship, or prohibiting the free exercise of religion, . . ."

It was in the conference committee of both the House and Senate, which was chaired by Madison, that the present language was drafted. During House debate, Madison contended that the clause should make clear that "Congress should not establish a religion, and enforce the legal observation of it by law, nor compel men to worship God in any Manner contrary to their conscience." Madison's intent was to deter religious persecution and prevent the government from establishing a national religion, but not necessarily to prohibit governmental encouragement of religion, in general.

On September 25, 1789, Congress transmitted to the state legislatures twelve proposed amendments to the U.S. Constitution. Ten of those amendments—the "Bill of Rights"—were adopted and ratified on December 15, 1791.

The First Amendment

The First Amendment to the United States Constitution states that "Congress shall make no law respecting an establishment of religion, or prohibiting the free exercise thereof." The first part of this clause is known as the "establishment clause," and the second part of this clause is known as the "free exercise clause."

The establishment clause prohibits the government from passing legislation to establish an official religion or preferring one religion over another. It enforces the concept of "separation of church and state." The free exercise clause prohibits the government, in most instances, from interfering with an individual's practice of their religion.

The Supreme Court is given the responsibility of interpreting the extent of the protection afforded these rights. The First Amendment has been interpreted by the Court as applying to the entire federal government even though it is only expressly applicable to Congress.

In addition, the Court has interpreted the Due Process clause of the Fourteenth Amendment, which was ratified on July 9, 1868, as protecting the rights in the First Amendment from interference by state governments. The Fourteenth Amendment to the United States Constitution states that "No

State shall ... deprive any person of life, liberty, or property, without due process of law ... "

The religious liberty guaranteed by the First Amendment has been called America's "first liberty." This concept of religious liberty includes: (i) freedom of conscience for people of all faiths or no faith; (ii) its guarantee as an inalienable right beyond the control of the state, and without governmental coercion; and (iii) the right to freely practice any religion or no religion.

A Directory of Religious Freedom Organizations is set forth in Appendix 1.

Religion and Politics

Although the First Amendment calls for a separation of church from state, it does not intend to exclude religion, and religious groups, from the public realm. In fact, many religious groups use a public platform to advocate their moral beliefs and concerns, and their right to do so is constitutionally protected.

Nevertheless, while religious opinions in public or political debate are protected under the "free exercise" clause, religious organizations that are exempt from taxation under Section 501 (c) (3) of the Internal Revenue Code are prohibited from engaging in partisan politics, i.e., endorsing a particular candidate for public office.

CHAPTER 2:

THE ROLE OF THE SUPREME COURT

In General

As stated earlier, the framer's objectives in drafting the freedom of religion clauses was not to prevent a general governmental encouragement of religion, but to deter religious persecution and preclude the establishment of a particular religion. Nevertheless, the Supreme Court, which is given the responsibility of interpreting the extent of constitutional protection, has long since abandoned this earlier interpretation of the religion clauses.

In *Everson v. Board of Education*, 330 U.S. 1, 15 (1947), the Court declared that the establishment clause forbids not only practices that "aid one religion" or "prefer one religion over another," but also those practices that "aid all religions." This view endures today, although the dissent has attempted to substitute the earlier view which holds that the religion clauses—and in particular, the establishment clause—seek to prevent "preferential" governmental promotion of some religions, while allowing governmental promotion of all religion in general. *Wallace v. Jaffree*, 472 U.S. 38, 91 (1985).

Despite this apparent contradiction between the historical intent of the religion clauses, and the evolved perspective that governmental endorsement of religion is prohibited, the latter remains the contemporary view. *Lee v. Weisman*, 112 S. Ct. 2649, 2678, 2683-84 (1992).

The Establishment Clause

"Congress shall make no law respecting *an establishment* of religion, or prohibiting the free exercise thereof..."

Following a long line of Supreme Court cases, a three-part objective test emerged to determine establishment clause validity of a particular law. In *Abington School District v. Schempp*, 374 U.S. 203, 222 (1963), the Court established the first two parts, considering both (i) the purpose; and (ii) the primary effect of the law. The Court held that if either the purpose or primary effect of the legislation was to advance or inhibit religion, then the law exceeded the scope of legislative power, and was invalid.

The third part of the test was stated in *Walz v. Tax Commission*, 397 U.S. 664, 674-75 (1970), wherein the Court held that a governmental program is impermissible if it results in "an excessive government entanglement with religion." "Excessive entanglement" was basically defined as involvement which called for official and continuing surveillance by the state.

The Lemon Test

In 1971, these three tests—(I) purpose; (ii) primary effect; and (iii) excessive entanglement—were combined and restated in *Lemon v. Kurtzman*, 403 U.S. 602, 612-13 (1971). The "Lemon test" is frequently cited in cases involving religion and public education, and has become the standard by which establishment clause cases are decided.

Nevertheless, the Court has refused to apply the Lemon test under limited circumstances. For example, in *Marsh v. Chambers*, 463 U.S. 783 (1983), the Court upheld legislative prayers on the basis of historical practice. However, in *Lee v. Weisman*, 112 S. Ct. 2649, at 2663 (1992), the Court stated that *Marsh* was the only case out of the thirty-one establishment clause cases heard between 1971 and 1992 which did not apply the Lemon test.

It has been proposed that "neutral" accommodations of religion should be allowed provided there is no coercion or attempt to establish a state religion. *Westside Community Board of Education v. Mergens*, 496 U.S. 226, 260-61. However, a substitute for the Lemon test has not yet been introduced.

The Free Exercise Clause

"Congress shall make no law respecting an establishment of religion, or prohibiting *the free exercise* thereof . . ."

In *Braunfeld v. Brown*, 366 U.S. 599, 607 (1961), the Court held that the free exercise clause prevents government from exerting any restraint on the free exercise of religion, and laws that target a particular religion, or religions in general, are unconstitutional.

Further, case law following *Braunfield* has consistently held that the free exercise clause bars governmental regulation of religious beliefs. The Court has held that individuals have an absolute right to maintain any religious beliefs they desire, as well as the right to maintain no religious belief whatsoever.

Nevertheless, because the practice of religion involves actions as well as ideology, the Court has not been so consistent in its rulings regarding religiously motivated conduct. The free exercise clause does not necessarily prevent the government from prohibiting certain actions simply because an expression of religion is the underlying motive. In addition, the free exercise clause does not prohibit the government from requiring certain conduct, regardless of a religious belief that proscribes such actions.

The Mormon Cases

The Court first addressed conduct and the free exercise clause in a series of cases involving the Mormons. The federal government sought to prosecute and convict members of the Church who committed bigamy and polygamy, claiming it was protected under their right to practice their religion. Convictions, however, were difficult to obtain because of the large number of Mormons who served as jurors and were reluctant to convict a fellow Mormon.

Thus, in 1882, Congress enacted a statute which barred "bigamists," "polygamists," and "any person cohabiting with more than one woman" from voting or serving on juries. Prospective voters were required to swear that they were neither bigamists nor polygamists, and to further state that they were not members of "any order, organization or association which teaches, advises, counsels or encourages its members, devotees or any other person to commit the crime of bigamy or polygamy . . . or which practices bigamy, polygamy or plural or celestial marriage as a doctrinal rite of such organization."

The Supreme Court found that this requirement was constitutional, and further sustained the government's revocation of the Mormon Church charter and confiscation of all church property not actually used for religious worship. *Davis v. Beason*, 133 U.S. 333 (1890); and *The Late Corporation of the Church of Jesus Christ of Latter-Day Saints v. United States*, 136 U.S. 1 (1890).

The Jehovah's Witnesses Cases

The religious denomination known as Jehovah's Witnesses generated a number of Court decisions involving their right to proselytize and otherwise publicly advocate their religious beliefs. In *Martin v. City of Struthers*, 319 U.S. 141 (1943), the Court struck down a city ordinance that made it unlawful for anyone distributing literature to summon residents from their homes to receive literature, a law particularly targeted at the religious group.

In general, the Court upheld licensing requirements for meetings held in public areas, providing that the groups must meet the "time, place, and manner" requirements which it held were not discriminatory in purpose, and did not seek to regulate religious speech.

The Court appears to have settled on a belief-conduct analysis in deciding these cases, under which religiously motivated conduct is not entitled to special protection. Although laws may not target religiously motivated conduct for unfavorable treatment, neutral laws which apply to the general population may regulate religious conduct—as well as other forms of conduct—regardless of the adverse effect the laws may have on religious exercise. The end result is that religious conduct is guaranteed equal—but not substantive—protection.

Government Neutrality in Religious Disputes.

Both religion clauses seek to enforce governmental neutrality in deciding controversies arising out of religious disputes. The Supreme Court has held that to permit the Court to resolve doctrinal disputes would jeopardize First Amendment principles.

For example, disputes may occur among churches over control of church property, particularly where a disassociation of one faction from the other occurs. Such a dispute often ends up in litigation. The religion clauses prevent governmental inquiry into religious doctrine in settling these disputes—i.e., making a determination that one church's religious doctrine should win over the other.

The Court is thus required to make its ruling according to the established decision-making process of the particular Church. For example, if action is taken according to majority vote, then the result of that vote would be binding.

A court confronted with a church property dispute is permitted to apply "neutral principles of law, developed for use in all property disputes," when to do so would not require resolution of doctrinal issues. *Presbyterian Church v. Hull Memorial Presbyterian Church*, 393 U.S. 440, 447, 449, 450-451 (1969); *Maryland and Virginia Eldership of the Churches of God v. Church of God of Sharpsburg*, 396 U.S. 367, 368 (1970).

In one case, the Court refused to interpret a church constitution to make an independent determination on the power of the church to reorganize its dioceses, holding that this was an internal church matter which was not subject to review by the Court. *The Serbian Eastern Orthodox Diocese v. Dionisije Milivojevich*, 426 U.S. 697, 720-25 (1976).

However, in *Jones v. Wolf*, 443 U.S. 595 (1979), a divided Court, while formally following the aforementioned principles, appeared to deviate from their application. In *Jones*, a dispute had developed in a local church, which was a member of a hierarchical church. The majority of the local church voted to withdraw from the general church. The proper authority of the general church determined that the minority vote actually constituted the "true congregation," and awarded the minority group authority over the local church.

In making its decision, the state court applied neutral principles by examining the church property deeds, state statutes, and the church constitution, and held that no language of trust in favor of the general church was contained in any of the items examined, and thus the property belonged to the local church.

The Supreme Court upheld the state court's decision. The dissent, however, argued that permitting the court to view only the church documents relating to property ownership in reaching its decision ignored the fact that the dispute was over ecclesiastical matters.

Financial Assistance to Religious Institutions

Although the framers of the religion clauses perceived financial support and sponsorship of religious activities as violative of the establishment clause, the Supreme Court has not denied all financial assistance to church-related institutions. A more detailed discussion of religion and public education is set forth in Chapter 4.

A chart of the significant Supreme Court First Amendment decisions involving Religion and Public Education is set forth at Appendix 2.

The Religious Freedom Restoration Act (RFRA)

In October 1993, Congress passed the Religious Freedom Restoration Act of 1993 (RFRA). The RFRA was sponsored by a coalition of religious leaders from many mainstream faiths, including Protestant, Catholic, Jewish, and Muslim. The Act sought to restore protections to most mainstream religious groups in the United States, including the traditional reading of the free exercise clause which provided that: (i) the government must show a compelling interest to justify any substantial restriction on religion; and (ii) the law must be the "least restrictive" means of furthering that interest.

Congress passed the RFRA in response to the U.S. Supreme Court's decision in *Employment Division of Oregon v. Smith*, 494 U.S. 872 (1990). In *Smith*, the Court held that laws not directed at religion are constitutional even if they adversely affect persons who are attempting to practice their religions.

The City of Boerne

On February 19, 1997, the U.S. Supreme Court heard a challenge to the constitutionality of the RFRA in the case of *The City of Boerne, Texas v. P.F. Flores, Archbishop of San Antonio.* In *Boerne,* the City refused to give a permit to St. Peter's Catholic Church allowing it to rebuild and expand a part of its church to accommodate the large increase in its membership. The City's reasons were that the church's facade was within its historic district and thus subject to its historic district law.

Church leaders brought suit under the RFRA in federal court claiming that the historic district law was unconstitutional and violated the RFRA as an infringement on religious exercise. The federal trial judge agreed and ruled that the RFRA was unconstitutional because it infringed on the court's authority to establish standards for evaluating constitutional issues.

The Fifth Circuit Court of Appeals reversed, holding that the RFRA was constitutional because the law did not usurp the judiciary's power to interpret the Constitution. In fact, the court held that the RFRA simply created additional rights and protections above the constitutional rights already recognized by the courts.

Both sides asked the U.S. Supreme Court to review the holding and decide whether the Constitution permitted Congress to legislate in this area. In passing the RFRA, Congress relied on its power under Section 5 of the Fourteenth Amendment to adopt laws designed to enforce individual rights, which states:

> The Congress shall have power to enforce, by appropriate legislation, the provisions of this article.

Although the Court had on many occasions examined the power given Congress under Section 5, it had not yet clearly stated the limits placed on that authority.

In this instance, the majority ruled that Congress exceeded its power under Section 5 when it passed the RFRA. The majority further stated that while legislation designed to prospectively prevent violations of individual freedom can in some instances be considered "enforcement" under Section 5, and thus constitutional, the scope of the law may not outweigh the nature of the violations. The majority concluded that the RFRA was too broad, particularly considering that there was no evidence that states were making any widespread efforts to restrict religious freedom.

Thus, the Supreme Court struck down this attempt by Congress to provide broad protection for persons practicing their religions. In doing so, the Court appears to have held that Congress may not enact legislation that provides freedoms or rights above and beyond those set forth in the Constitution.

The text of the Religious Freedom Restoration Act is set forth at Appendix 3.

CHAPTER 3:

RELIGION IN THE WORKPLACE

Overview

Because the First Amendment to the United States Constitution is directed only at governmental activities which interfere with religious freedom, it has no jurisdiction over nongovernmental employers and offers no protection for their employees.

Nevertheless, recourse for religious discrimination in employment may be found under a variety of state and federal laws. Religious employment discrimination refers to the illegal practice of making employment decisions, such as hiring and promotion, based on an employee's religious preferences. Private employers, as well as state and local governments and public or private educational institutions, employment agencies, labor unions, and apprentice programs are subject to anti-discrimination laws.

Title VII of the Civil Rights Act of 1964

The Equal Employment Opportunity Commission (EEOC) was established by Title VII of the Civil Rights Act of 1964. The EEOC interprets and enforces the major federal anti-discrimination laws, including Title VII of the Civil Rights Act of 1964 (Title VII). Title VII prohibits discrimination in hiring, promotion, discharge, pay, fringe benefits, and other aspects of employment, on the basis of religion, among other protected classes. Title VII covers both current employees and job applicants.

Under Title VII, an employer is also required to accommodate an employee's religious practices—e.g. Sabbath and religious holiday observances—provided the practices do not cause undue hardship on the employer.

Title VII also outlaws the promotion of a hostile work environment. "Hostile work environment" is a term which describes hostile behaviors to which an employee is subjected in the workplace. For example, a hostile work environment may be found where there exists a pattern of religious slurs or jokes.

Unlike discrimination in hiring, firing and terms of employment, the creation of a hostile work environment is usually accomplished by the acts of non-management employees. However, management can be held liable if the victim can show proof that management had knowledge of the harassment and did nothing to stop it.

Suspected violations of Title VII should be reported to the United States Equal Employment Opportunity Commission (EEOC) located at 1801 L Street, N.W., Washington, DC 20507. An EEOC field office can be located by calling 800-669-EEOC. Individuals who are hearing impaired may dial the EEOC's TDD number, 800-800-3302.

State Employment Discrimination Statutes

Many state statutes provide additional protection for victims of religious employment discrimination. Some of these laws are patterned after the federal statute, and provide similar protection to workers employed by those employers not covered under the federal statute.

The reader is advised to also check the law of his or her own jurisdiction concerning religious discrimination in employment, as many states provide protection against such discrimination, and may impose even stricter requirements on employers than the federal law.

The Role of Religion in the Federal Workplace

In August 1997, President Clinton issued a directive and established federal guidelines on the role of religion in the federal workplace. In an effort to reaffirm the right to religious freedom, the President directed the heads of the federal executive departments and agencies to comply with the Federal Guidelines on Religious Exercise and Religious Expression in the Federal Workplace. The President called for strict adherence to these guidelines to ensure that federal agencies respect the rights of those who engage in religious practices or espouse religious beliefs, as well as those who reject religion altogether.

The text of the Federal Guidelines on Religious Exercise and Expression in the Federal Workplace is set forth at Appendix 4.

Scope of Coverage

The federal guidelines apply to all civilian executive branch agencies, officials, and employees in the federal workplace. The guidelines address the federal employees' right to engage in religious exercise and religious expression when the employees are acting in their personal capacity within the federal workplace.

The guidelines do not comprehensively address whether and when the government and its employees may engage in religious speech directed at the public. The guidelines do not address religious exercise and religious expression by uniformed military personnel, or chaplains employed by the federal government, nor do they address or define the rights and responsibilities of non-governmental employers and their employees.

In particular, the guidelines establish the following principles:

Personal Religious Expression

Federal agencies are required to allow their employees to engage in personal religious expression to the greatest extent possible, although an agency may restrict any speech that truly interferes with its ability to perform public services. However, when an agency allows nonreligious speech, an agency must also usually allow similar speech of a religious nature.

The one exception to this neutrality principle is when religious speech would lead a reasonable observer to conclude that the government is endorsing religion, as prohibited by the establishment clause.

Employment Discrimination

The federal government may not discriminate in employment on the basis of religion. This means that an agency may not hire or refuse to hire, promote or refuse to promote, or otherwise favor or disfavor a potential, current, or former employee because of his or her religion or religious beliefs. Further, an agency, or any supervisor within an agency, may not coerce an employee to participate in religious activities—or to refrain from participating in otherwise permissible religious activities—by offering better, or threatening worse, employment conditions. In addition, an agency must prevent any supervisor or any employee from engaging in religious harassment or creating, through the use of intimidation or pervasive or severe ridicule or insult, a religiously hostile environment.

Accommodation of Religious Practices

Agencies are required to reasonably accommodate their employees' religious practices—e.g., when work schedules interfere with Sabbath or other religious holiday observances or when work rules prevent an employee from wearing religiously compelled dress.

Although workplace efficiency may be a factor, an agency must always accommodate an employee's religious practices in the absence of nonspeculative costs, and may need to accommodate such practice even when doing so will impose some hardship on the agency's operations.

CHAPTER 4:

RELIGION IN PUBLIC EDUCATION

In General

The relationship between church and state in the public school setting is an often litigated area. The goal of the First Amendment in public education is to create an educational setting that is neutral on religion—i.e., no particular religious doctrine is promoted, and non-believers are afforded the same protections.

To make sure that the government does not encourage individuals to join a particular religious group, the religion clauses provide for the separation of church and state. Thus, the government is not permitted to financially support any particular religious group, and does not proclaim an official religion.

In a recent statement of principles, a number of religious, civic and educational groups agreed to the following role of religious liberty in the public schools:

> Public schools may not inculcate nor inhibit religion. They must be places where religion and religious conviction are treated with fairness and respect. Public schools uphold the First Amendment when they protect the religious liberty rights of students of all faiths or none. Schools demonstrate fairness when they ensure that the curriculum includes study about religion, where appropriate, as an important part of a complete education.

Religious Expression

Schools must respect the right of students to engage in religious activity and discussion. In general, individual students are permitted to read the Bible and pray, and engage in a discussion of their religious beliefs, provided their behavior is neither coercive nor disruptive. Students also have the right to express their religious views during a class discussion, or as part of an assignment, where relevant to the subject matter.

The text of the Presidential Directive on Religious Expression in Public Schools is set forth at Appendix 5.

School Prayer

The sponsorship of school prayer and Bible reading have been declared unconstitutional under the establishment clause of the First Amendment, even if there is voluntary participation. The U.S. Supreme Court has held that voluntary participation does not diminish the constitutional violation because the primary effect of such activity is to advance religion, even if the nature of the observance is non-denominational. Thus, school officials are prohibited from sponsoring, or otherwise participating in, student prayer or other religious activities.

Students are free to pray alone or in groups, provided they are not coercive or disruptive, and do not intrude upon the rights of other students. Further, these activities must be voluntary and initiated by the students, not school-sponsored.

In addition, state laws which promote silent meditation have been similarly struck down as violating the establishment clause. The U.S. Supreme Court held that the proposed "moment of silence" was intended to convey a preference for students to engage in devotional activities.

Graduation Prayers

In its 1992 ruling in *Lee v. Weisman*, the U.S. Supreme Court also held that graduation prayers are unconstitutional in public schools even if the prayer is student-led and supported by a majority of the student body. Nevertheless, individual students have the constitutional right to pray as long as they don't disrupt educational activities, or try to coerce other students to pray with them.

Student Religious Clubs

Under the federal Equal Access Act, as further discussed below, secondary public schools receiving federal funds must allow students to form religious clubs if the school allows other noncurriculum-related clubs —i.e., any club not directly related to courses offered by the school—to meet during noninstructional time. Student religious clubs may have access to school facilities and media on the same basis as other noncurriculum-related student clubs.

School Curriculum

There have been ongoing disputes over the content of curriculum that touches on aspects of religion. Although the Supreme Court has banned school prayer and Bible reading in the classroom, the influences religion has had on history, literature and philosophy may be taught.

The Supreme Court has indicated many times that teaching about religion, as distinguished from religious indoctrination, is an important part of a complete education. The study of religion may be placed in the curriculum wherever it naturally arises.

Religious holidays also offer opportunities to teach about religion in elementary and secondary schools. Teaching about religious holidays, which is permissible, is different from celebrating religious holidays, which is prohibited, and educates children about the history and traditions of various cultures.

The Court has held that the performance of sacred music is permissible as part of the school's academic program provided it is not used to promote a particular religious belief. School concerts that present a variety of selections may include religious music.

Teachers are required to teach religious topics in an objective manner, and are prohibited from proselytizing or otherwise imposing their own personal religious or non-religious beliefs on the students. If questioned on this issue, a teacher may advise the students that he or she prefers to keep her religious beliefs private, or may respond without promoting any religious belief. In addition, teachers are generally not permitted to inquire about the religious beliefs of their students, although students may express their own religious views as they relate to the discussion being held.

Creationism

Some states have passed laws requiring that the creationist theory, which is based on the biblical account, be taught in the science classroom. However, courts have generally found these laws to be unconstitutional on the ground that they promote a particular religious view. The Supreme Court has, however, conceded that a variety of scientific theories concerning the origin of mankind can be appropriately taught in the science classroom provided the underlying intent is clearly secular.

Religious Apparel

Students who must wear religious apparel to comply with their religious beliefs should be permitted to do so in school. In addition, students are also entitled to display religious symbols on their clothing to the same extent that other non-religious messages are allowed.

School Holidays

Certain religious holiday activities have been permitted in the educational setting, such as Christmas, Easter and Chanukah activities, because they have become secular customs that people of many different backgrounds and religions celebrate.

Baccalaureate Ceremonies

Although public schools may not sponsor religious baccalaureate ceremonies, parents and community groups are permitted to sponsor such services for students who wish to attend. The school may announce the baccalaureate in the same way it announces other community events. If the school allows community groups to rent or otherwise use its facilities after-hours, then a privately sponsored baccalaureate may be held on campus under the same terms offered to any private group.

Distribution of Religious Literature

Generally, students have a right to distribute religious literature on public school grounds subject to time, place and manner restrictions imposed by the school. These restrictions should be reasonable and must apply equally to the distribution of any non-school student literature. Nevertheless, public schools may prohibit the distribution of certain literature absolutely, such as material which is obscene or defamatory.

Released Time

Public schools are permitted to allow released time programs off school grounds for the purpose of accommodating the needs of religious students. However, the schools may not encourage or discourage participation, and may not penalize students on the basis of whether they attend or not.

The Role of the School District

Public schools are prohibited from either promoting or denigrating any religion, or the lack of religious belief. In such a pluralistic society, school districts must develop policies concerning religious issues in order to further religious liberty and instruct teachers and administrators on the role of religion and public education.

To illustrate how different communities have addressed these issues, a sample school district policy on religious issues in public education is set forth at Appendix 6.

Public Support of Private Schools

Although the framers of the First Amendment perceived financial support and sponsorship of religious activities as violative of the establishment clause, the Supreme Court has not denied all financial assistance to church-related institutions.

For example, in *Bradfield v. Roberts* 175 U.S. 291 (1899), the Court made its first ruling in this area when it validated a government grant for a Catholic hospital. In the Court's opinion, the hospital was a secular institution, not a religious institution.

However, in ruling on the subject of whether the government can provide free transportation for parochial school children, the Court took a more narrow view, stating that "Neither a state nor the Federal Government can . . . pass laws which aid one religion, aid all religions, or prefer one religion over another . . . ." Nevertheless, the Court majority decided to sustain the transportation provision for parochial school students, holding that the transportation was a form of "public welfare legislation" which benefitted the child.

This "child benefit theory" later was relied upon to authorize textbook loan programs for parochial students in *Board of Education v. Allen*, 392 U.S. 236 (1968). The Court reasoned that loaning the textbooks was secular in that it furthered the educational opportunities of children and, since the books were merely on loan, the state retained ownership of the books, and the parochial schools did not thereby obtain any financial benefit.

In the cases that followed, the Court has generally ruled that legislation which involves religion may be sustained if there is a secular purpose—i.e., a legitimate, non-sectarian basis for government assistance to religious schools. However, the state must be careful to avoid assisting the religious goals of these schools, either directly or indirectly.

The Court will look at the extent to which the religious mission of the school is interwoven with the secular purpose. Nevertheless, public aid will not be denied simply because the funds may increase the school's own budget, on the assumption that those funds will then be designated for religious purposes.

According to the National Center for Education Statistics (NCES), approximately one in four schools in the United States today are private schools, the overwhelming majority of which are religion-related, e.g. Catholic schools. These schools are responsible for educating a significant percentage of the school-age population in the United States.

Recognizing that all children are entitled to benefit from federal programs, private school students, teachers, and other personnel are allowed to participate in a number of federal education programs. Most notable are the services available under the "Improving America's Schools Act of 1994" (IASA) which, among other things, benefit educationally needy elementary and secondary students living in areas with high concentrations of children from low-income families.

Private schools receive no direct aid from these programs. Program funds are granted to public authorities, usually the local education agency (LEA), who is responsible for serving eligible students, teachers, and other personnel within their boundaries, whether they attend public or private school.

To ensure that private school students, teachers, and other personnel have every opportunity to participate in federal education programs for which they are eligible, private school officials are advised to contact their local public school district and ask for the person in charge of coordinating federal education programs.

The location of instructional services provided to private school children under the Act is limited by the U.S. Supreme Court's decision in *Aguilar v. Felton*, 473 U.S. 402 (1985). In *Aguilar*, the Court held that it is unconstitutional for public school personnel to provide instruction in religiously-affiliated private schools.

The Supreme Court ruled that instructional services by private school teachers to religious school children in religious school buildings constituted "excessive entanglement" between government and religion in violation of the First Amendment of the U.S. Constitution.

The LEA is required to provide eligible private school children with available services under the Act, which must be equitable in comparison to services and other benefits provided public school participants. However, the delivery options selected must be in compliance with the holding in the U.S. Supreme Court case, *Aguilar*, as discussed above.

In the case of children attending religiously affiliated private schools, several court cases, most notably the *Aguilar* case, have dealt with the manner in which these children may be served in light of constitutional requirements contained in the First Amendment. Most significant is the prohibition in *Aguilar* against personnel providing instructional services in religiously affiliated schools. Because of this prohibition, an LEA must provide equitable services through alternate delivery methods.

Delivery options in providing services to participating private school children include, but are not limited to:

Instructional services provided at a public school site or other public or privately owned neutral site;

Educational radio or television;

Computer-assisted instruction;

Extended-day services;

Home tutoring;

Take-home computers; and

Interactive technology.

Nevertheless, the Court has approved broad public assistance to religious institutions of higher learning. For example, the Court sustained construction grants to church-related colleges and universities. The Court found that the purpose and effect of the grants were secular and that, unlike elementary and secondary schools, religious colleges were not so permeated with religious indoctrination. The Court further held that the supervision required to ensure conformance with the non-religious use requirement did not constitute "excessive entanglement."

Statement of First Principles

A number of religious, educational and civic groups have joined together and drafted a document known as the "Statement of First Principles," which encompasses civic ground rules for addressing conflicts in public education. In their introduction to the Statement, the sponsors set forth their reasons for drafting this Statement, as follows:

> Our nation urgently needs a reaffirmation of our shared commitment, as American citizens, to the guiding principles of the Religious Liberty clauses of the First Amendment to the Constitution. The rights and responsibilities of the Religious Liberty clauses provide the civic framework within which we are able to debate our differences, to understand one another, and to forge public policies that serve the common good in public education.
>
> Today, many American communities are divided over educational philosophy, school reform, and the role of religion and values in our public schools. Conflict and debate are vital to democracy. Yet, if controversies about public education are to advance the best interests of the nation, then how we debate, and not only what we debate, is critical.
>
> This Statement of Principles is not an attempt to ignore or minimize differences that are important and abiding, but rather a reaf-

firmation of what we share as American citizens across our differences. Democratic citizenship does not require a compromise of our deepest convictions.

We invite all men and women of good will to join us in affirming these principles and putting them into action. The time has come for us to work together for academic excellence, fairness, and shared civic values in our nation's schools.

The text of the Statement of First Principles is set forth at Appendix 7.

Sponsors

The following groups sponsored the Statement of First Principles:

The American Association of School Administrators (AASA) - AASA was founded in 1865, and is the professional organization for more than 16,500 educational leaders across North America and in many other countries. The four major focus areas for AASA are: (i) improving the condition of children and youth; (ii) preparing schools and school systems for the 21st century; (iii) connecting schools and communities; and (iv) enhancing the quality and effectiveness of school leaders. The AASA is one of elementary and secondary education's long-standing professional organizations.

The American Center for Law and Justice (ACLJ) - The ACLJ is a not-for-profit public interest law firm and educational organization dedicated to the promotion of pro-liberty, pro-life and pro-family causes. The Center engages in litigation, provides legal services, renders advice and counsel to clients, and supports attorneys who are involved in defending the religious and civil liberties of Americans. The ACLJ cooperates with other organizations that are committed to the defense of traditional values and serves the public through educational efforts concerning the First Amendment and religious freedom issues.

The American Federation of Teachers (AFT) - The AFT is a union which exists to serve the interests of its members as determined by democratic processes at the local, state and national levels.

The Anti-Defamation League (ADL) - The Anti-Defamation League, founded in 1913, is the world's leading organization fighting anti-Semitism through programs and services that counteract hatred, prejudice and bigotry. The mission of the Anti-Defamation League is "to stop the defamation of the Jewish people and to secure justice and fair treatment to all citizens alike."

The Association for Supervision and Curriculum Development (ASCD) - The ASCD, founded in 1943, is an international, nonprofit, nonpartisan education association committed to the mission of forging covenants in teaching and learning for the success of all learners.

The Carnegie Foundation for the Advancement of Teaching - The Carnegie Foundation for the Advancement of Teaching was chartered in 1906 by an Act of Congress. The foundation has worked closely with many institutions of higher learning in researching, writing and presenting work in various area of education.

The Catholic League for Religious and Civil Rights - The Catholic League, founded in 1973, is the nation's largest Catholic civil rights organization. The Catholic League works to safeguard both the religious freedom rights and the free speech rights of Catholics whenever and wherever they are threatened.

The Central Conference of American Rabbis (CCAR) - Founded in 1889, the CCAR is a body of rabbis who consider themselves, and are considered to be, the organized rabbinate of Reform Judaism.

The Christian Coalition - The Christian Coalition is a pro-family citizen action organization seeking to impact public policy on a local, state and national level, to teach Christians effective citizenship, and to promote Christian values in government.

Christian Educators Association International - The CEAI is a professional association for primarily public school educators who happen to be Christians by faith. The CEAI's stated mission is to "[e]ncourage, equip, and empower Christians serving in public and private schools."

The Christian Legal Society - The Christian Legal Society is a nationwide organization of Christian attorneys, law professors, judges and law students. Its legal advocacy arm is The Center for Law and Religious Freedom, which comprises a network of volunteer attorneys defending religious freedom in their communities, in the high courts and in Congress.

Citizens for Excellence in Education (CEE) - Citizens for Excellence in Education is a Christian organization focused on the protection of children. CEE believes in returning traditional moral values, grounded in the Judeo-Christian ethic on which the United States was founded, to the classroom.

The Council on Islamic Education - The Council on Islamic Education is a national nonprofit resource organization for K-12 educators, school division publishers, education officials and policymakers, curriculum developers and other education professionals.

The First Amendment Center - The First Amendment Center is an organization which reports on significant issues affecting First Amendment rights.

The National Association of Elementary School Principals (NAESP) - The National Association of Elementary School Principals is a powerful advocate for K-8 principals and the 33 million children they serve. The more than 27,000 members receive a wide range of services aimed at helping principals do the best possible job in leading their schools to excellence, including professional development training programs

The National Association of Evangelicals (NAE) - The NAE serves the evangelical community through united action, cooperative ministry, and strategic planning. Its stated mission is to extend the kingdom of God through a fellowship of member denominations, churches, organizations and individuals.

The National Association of Secondary School Principals (NASSP) - Membership in National Association of Secondary School Principals includes a wide variety of people interested in secondary education.

The National Council of Churches - The National Council of Churches is a community of 33 member church bodies, including Protestant and Orthodox churches, which are related to more than 141,000 congregations across the country. The Council has long maintained programs dealing with religious and social issues.

The National Education Association (NEA) - The National Education Association is a volunteer-based organization supported by a network of staff at the local, state and national levels.

The National Parent Teacher Association - The National Parent Teacher Association is an organization whose mission is to: (i) to support and speak on behalf of children and youth in the schools, in the community, and before governmental bodies and other organizations that make decisions affecting children; (ii) to assist parents in developing the skills they need to raise and protect their children; and (iii) to encourage parental and public involvement in the public schools of this nation.

The National School Boards Association - The National School Boards Association is an organization that is dedicated to excellence and equity in public education through school board leadership.

People for the American Way - Founded in 1980 to monitor and counter the divisive agenda of the Religious Right political movement,

People For the American Way seeks to defend and strengthen vital institutions like our public education system and public broadcasting system and to protect individual and religious liberty.

Phi Delta Kappa - Phi Delta Kappa is an international professional fraternity for men and women in education. Members include classroom teachers, school administrators, college and university professors and educational specialists of many types. The purpose of Phi Delta Kappa is to promote quality education, with particular emphasis on publicly supported education.

The Union of American Hebrew Congregations (UAHC) - The Union of American Hebrew Congregations is the synagogue arm of the Reform movement whose mission is to: (i) establish a Hebrew theological institute; (ii) provide for and advance Sabbath schools for the instruction of the young; (iii) aid and encourage new and young congregations; and (iv) provide, sustain and manage such other institutions which will aid the common welfare and progress of Judaism.

A directory of the sponsors of the Statement of First Principles is set forth at Appendix 8.

The Equal Access Act

Congress, acknowledging the constitutional prohibition against government promotion of religion, also recognized that non-school-sponsored student speech, including religious speech, should not be eradicated from the school environment. In that connection, Congress passed The Equal Access Act on August 11, 1984, which applies only to public secondary schools that receive federal financial assistance.

In 1990, the constitutionality of The Equal Access Act was validated by the Supreme Court in *Westside Community Schools v. Mergens*. According to the Supreme Court, the primary purpose of Congress in passing the Act was to end "perceived widespread discrimination" against religious speech in public schools.

Basic Concepts

There are three basic concepts expressed in the Equal Access Act: (i) Nondiscrimination; (ii) Protection; and (iii) Local Control.

Nondiscrimination

If a public secondary school permits student groups to meet for student-initiated activities not directly related to the school curriculum, it is required to treat all such student groups equally. The school cannot discriminate against any student group "on the basis of the religious, political, philosophical, or other content of the speech at such meetings." Religious speech must receive equal treatment.

Protection

State-initiated or endorsed religious activities in public schools is unconstitutional. However, in validating the Equal Access Act, the Court noted that the "crucial difference between government speech endorsing religion, which the establishment clause forbids, and private speech endorsing religion, which the free speech and free exercise clauses protect."

Local Control

The Act does not limit the authority of the school to maintain order and discipline or to protect the well-being of students and faculty.

Noncurriculum-Related Student Groups

The Supreme Court has interpreted a "noncurriculum-related student group" to mean "any student group that does not directly relate to the body of courses offered by the school." According to the Court, a student group directly relates to a school's curriculum only if:

1. the subject matter of the group is actually taught, or will soon be taught, in a regularly offered course;

2. the subject matter of the group concerns the body of courses as a whole; or

3. participation in the group is required for a particular course or results in academic credit.

Schools may not substitute their own definition of "noncurriculum-related student group" for that of the Court. Local school authorities, subject to review by the courts, determine which student groups are, in fact, curriculum-related. However, the Supreme Court has made clear that a school cannot defeat the intent of the Act by defining "curriculum-related" in a way that arbitrarily results in only those student clubs approved by the school being allowed to meet.

The Act does not take away a school's authority to establish reasonable time, place, and manner regulations. The school may also assign the rooms in which student groups can meet, and may enforce order and discipline during the meetings. Nevertheless, the time, place, and manner and regulations must be uniform and nondiscriminatory. In addition, the prospective group must be student-initiated. "Student-initiated" means that the students themselves are seeking permission to meet and that they will direct and control the meeting.

In general, teachers or other school employees are usually required to be present during student meetings but are not permitted to participate in the activity. The Act also prohibits teachers or other school officials from influencing the form or content of any prayer or other religious activity that takes place. Nevertheless, school employees are not required to attend any meetings if the content of the speech at the meeting is contrary to the beliefs of the employee.

The following activities have been held not to constitute sponsorship of a student group activity:

1. Assignment of a teacher to a meeting for custodial purposes;

2. The expenditure of public funds for the incidental cost of providing the space for student-initiated meetings;

3. Payment to a teacher for monitoring a student religious club;

4. The use of school media to announce meetings of noncurriculum-related student groups. In fact, the Supreme Court has ruled that schools are required to allow student groups to use school media if the other non-curriculum-related student groups are allowed to use the school media.

Student groups that are unlawful, or that materially and substantially interfere with the orderly conduct of educational activities, may be excluded. However, a student group cannot be denied equal access simply because its ideas are unpopular or even repugnant to other students. The constitutional right of a particular student group to meet does not depend on other student's approval. All students enjoy the constitutional guarantee of free speech.

If a school violates The Equal Access Act, the aggrieved party has a remedy under the law. He or she may bring suit in a U.S. District Court to compel a school to observe the law. Although equal access violations will generally not result in the loss of federal funds, a school district could be liable for damages to a student group that prevails in a lawsuit brought under the Act, including an award of legal fees.

The text of the Equal Access Act is set forth at Appendix 9.

CHAPTER 5:

NATIVE AMERICAN RELIGIOUS RIGHTS

Historical Background

Despite persecution and adversity, Native Americans have attempted to maintain their traditional spiritual practices in a society dominated by Judeo-Christian values and beliefs. Native American religious practices were historically misunderstood and forbidden, and Christian missionaries considered such practices to be demonic.

The federal government tried to convert Native Americans to Christianity. However, the government soon realized that there was an inseparable connection between Native American spirituality and culture, which is guided by natural related occurrences, such as the seasons. After much persecution, U.S. policy in Indian affairs began to change, and the government sought to make amends by passing legislation designed to protect Native American religious practices.

The American Indian Religious Freedom Act of 1978 (AIRFA)

In 1978, in an effort to reverse the long history of government oppression of Native American tribal religious practices, Congress passed the American Indian Religious Freedom Act (AIRFA). The AIRFA was designed to guarantee constitutional First Amendment protection of freedom of religion for Native Americans, however, it failed to provide for any legal provisions for enforcement.

Thus, the AIRFA has been viewed more as a policy statement rather than a legally enforceable mandate with remedies. In fact, the Supreme Court interpreted the Act to merely require the government to consult or notify Native Americans when they intended to take any actions that would affect Native American religious practices.

The text of the American Indian Religious Freedom Act of 1978 is set forth at Appendix 10.

The American Indian Religious Freedom Act Amendments of 1994

On October 6, 1994, Congress passed the American Indian Religious Freedom Act Amendments of 1994, which basically amended the American Indian Religious Freedom Act of 1978 to provide for the traditional use of peyote by Indians for religious purposes. The Act further provides that prison authorities are neither required to permit—nor prohibited from permitting—access to peyote by Native Americans who are incarcerated in Federal or State prisons.

The text of the American Indian Religious Freedom Act Amendments of 1994 is set forth at Appendix 11.

Presidential Directive on Eagle Feather Distribution

Recognizing that eagle feathers hold a sacred place in Native American culture and religious practices, on April 29, 1994, President Clinton issued a directive concerning the practice of eagle feather distribution for Native American religious purposes.

The directive instructs federal agencies to work cooperatively with tribal governments in order to accommodate Native American religious practices to the fullest extent under the law. Further, all agencies responsible for managing federal lands are directed to improve their collection and transfer of eagle carcasses and eagle body parts for Native American religious purposes to the National Eagle Repository.

The U.S. Department of Interior is responsible for ensuring the priority of distribution of eagles for Native American religious purposes, and expanding efforts to involve Native American tribes, organizations, and individuals in the distribution process.

Native American Prisoners

Native Americans incarcerated in American prisons have generally been denied the right to practice their religion, despite the fact that accommodations are routinely made for the practices of many other mainstream religions. Courts quickly dismiss most religious freedom claims brought by Native American prisoners, with little consideration to the merits of their claims.

Because Native American religious practices differ so greatly from mainstream practices, prison officials generally view these practices—e.g., the use of eagle feathers—with suspicion. However, these rituals are no more suspect than those performed in America's mainstream religions—e.g., the taking of communion, and the wearing of crosses and scapulas, etc. This misunderstanding stems from the failure to educate prison employees about religious practices outside of the accepted mainstream religions.

Much of the concern over the rights of Native Americans prisoners also stems from the fact that statistics demonstrate that Native Americans are disproportionately represented in the prison population. According to a

1984 study by the National Minority Advisory Council on Criminal Justice, Native American arrest rates were eleven times higher than those of whites and three times higher than those of blacks. In addition, Native Americans serve thirty-five percent more time in prison than non-Indians who commit similar offenses before they are eligible for parole. Further, Native American defendants have historically plead guilty in court in order to avoid confrontation.

CHAPTER 6:

THE WILLIAMSBURG CHARTER

In an effort to return to "first principles," the Williamsburg Charter was drafted by a coalition of members of America's leading faiths—Protestant, Catholic, Jewish, and secularist—and revised over the course of two years in close consultation with political, academic, educational, and religious leaders.

The Williamsburg Charter was written and published primarily to address the dilemmas, challenges, and opportunities posed by religious liberty in modern-day American life. The stated purposes of the charter are to: (i) celebrate the uniqueness of the First Amendment religious liberty clauses; (ii) reaffirm religious liberty—or freedom of conscience—for citizens of all faiths and none; (iii) set out the place of religious liberty within American public life; and (iv) define the guiding principles by which people with deep differences can contend robustly but civilly in the public arena.

The Charter was named after Williamsburg, in honor of the city's role as the cradle of religious liberty in America. It was signed in 1988 by former Presidents Gerald Ford and Jimmy Carter, by the two living chief justices of the United States, and by nearly 200 national leaders from political, academic, educational, and religious backgrounds.

In signing, these individuals strongly reaffirmed the principles of religious liberty that are essential for developing a common vision for the common good. As set forth in the introduction:

> "The Charter sets forth a renewed national compact, in the sense of a solemn mutual agreement between parties, on how we view the place of religion in American life and how we should contend with each other's deepest differences in the public sphere. It is a call to a vision of public life that will allow conflict to lead to consensus, religious commitment to reinforce political civility. In this way, diversity is not a point of weakness but a source of strength."

The Charter sets forth the guiding principles that emerge from the First Amendment religion clauses that religious liberty is a fundamental and inalienable right, and that individuals and groups are responsible for guarding the religious liberty rights of others as if they were their own. In that connection, the Charter states, in part:

> "We affirm that a right for one is a right for another and a responsibility for all. A right for a Protestant is a right for an Eastern Ortho-

dox is a right for a Catholic is a right for a Jew is a right for a Humanist is a right for a Mormon is a right for a Muslim is a right for a Buddhist, and for the followers of any other faith within the wide bounds of the republic."

The text of the Williamsburg Charter is set forth at Appendix 12.

CHAPTER 7:

MISCELLANEOUS ISSUES

Religion and Child Custody Issues

There are many contested issues involved in child custody litigation. Reaching a decision may be further complicated when the religious upbringing of the child becomes an issue in the dispute.

Controversy over the religious upbringing of a child introduces constitutional considerations into the proceedings. The court is called upon to balance the religious rights of the parents and child, while constrained by the Fourteenth Amendment which makes applicable to the state judiciary the First Amendment prohibition against the making of law respecting an establishment of religion, or prohibiting its free exercise.

The court is clearly not permitted to favor one religion over another in making a custody determination. However, the court may consider whether a particular religion maintains practices which are harmful to the child. Further, a court may consider whether a particular religion has been an important factor in the child's life, and whether such continuity is in the best interests of the child. This deliberation does not require the court to make a value judgment concerning any particular religion.

In general, a custodial parent in a sole custody situation has the right to determine the child's religious upbringing. However, this does not preclude the noncustodial parent from exposing the child to his or her religion, unless there is some indication of harm to the child. This reasoning would likely be followed in joint custody situations where the parents are unable to cooperate in a decision on the child's religious upbringing. Parents may also agree, in writing, as to the religious upbringing of the child.

Religion and Prisoners' Rights

Prisoner claims of religious freedom violations generally rely on the free exercise clause of the First Amendment, which basically guarantees the right to believe, or not believe, in any religion, but does not necessarily protect the right to engage in all religion-related conduct.

The Supreme Court has acknowledged that prisoners are still entitled to their First Amendment rights even though they have been convicted of a crime and sentenced to prison, including the right to free exercise of religion. Nevertheless, the Court has held that the constitutional rights of prisoners must be balanced against the objectives of the prison system—e.g., deterrence of crime, rehabilitation of prisoners, and security concerns—because incarceration necessarily results in a limitation of a number of privileges and rights.

In 1987, the Supreme Court set forth the appropriate test in determining free exercise violations brought by prisoners. The majority held that as long as the prison rule or regulation was "reasonably related" to legitimate penalogical interests, a prisoner's constitutional claim would fail. Clearly, this is an insurmountable burden to overcome. In accordance with this balancing of interests test, the Supreme Court has basically directed that courts defer to the judgment of prison administrators in deciding religious rights cases brought by prisoners (the "deference doctrine").

The dissent's view that prison officials must offer proof that the rule or regulation is "necessary to further an important governmental interest" and that the limitations on freedoms should be "no greater than necessary to effectuate the governmental objective involved" was rejected. Thus, under the current law, it is unlikely that a prisoner will be victorious in the majority of free exercise claims and, in many courts, the prison official merely has to proffer some safety concern, however speculative, to prevail.

Religion and Medical Issues

Some religions prohibit their members from seeking medical treatment on religious grounds, e.g., Jehovah's Witnesses. In general, most states do not intervene when a competent adult refuses medical treatment. Nevertheless, under some circumstances, the state will intervene. For example, if an adult's refusal of relatively minor medical treatment, such as a blood transfusion, will lead to his or her death, and result in his or her children becoming orphaned, most states will intervene to prevent the children from becoming wards of the state. However, where such intervention is deemed to be without justification, the individual may be able to bring a lawsuit against the responsible parties.

The state will use a "best interests of the child" approach when considering whether a minor is in need of medical treatment. In such a case, the state will intervene and require medical care, regardless of the wishes of the parents, and will generally appoint a guardian to made medical decisions on behalf of the child. Some jurisdictions will hold parents criminally liable under child neglect and endangerment statutes if they refuse to provide necessary medical treatment to their children, even if their refusal is based on religious grounds.

Priest-Penitent Privilege

Under the common law, there existed a confidentiality privilege relating to communications between a priest and an individual seeking counseling from the priest. An individual's right to confidentiality of communications made with a member of the clergy has been codified by almost every state. Generally, in order to claim this privilege, the communication must be made to one who is recognized as a minister or member of the clergy, in his or her professional capacity, with an expectation of privacy.

The privilege is usually held by the individual who seeks counseling, however, it may be lost if that individual permits a third party to attend the session. Jurisdictions are split on whether the clergy member has a right to divulge information under extenuating circumstances, e.g., confessions of child abuse, or potential harm to a third party. In addition, some jurisdictions permit an individual to file a lawsuit against a clergy member who violates their confidentiality under an invasion of privacy or breach of fiduciary duty theory.

APPENDICES

APPENDIX 1:

DIRECTORY OF RELIGIOUS FREEDOM ORGANIZATIONS

ORGANIZATION	ADDRESS	TELEPHONE NUMBER	FAX NUMBER	E-MAIL	INTERNET WEBSITE
American Atheists	P.O. Box 140195, Austin, Texas 78714-0195	512-458-1244	512-467-9525	info@atheists.org	http://www.atheists.org/
American Civil Liberties Union	132 West 43rd Street, New York, New York 10036	212-944-9800	212-869-9065	infoaclu@aclu.org	http://www.aclu.org/
ACLU of Wisconsin	207 E. Buffalo Street, Suite 325, Milwaukee, Wisconsin 53202-5712	414-272-4032	414-272-0182	acluwisc@mail.execpc.com	http://www.acluwi.org/
American Jewish Congress	15 East 84th Street, New York, New York 10028-0458	212-879-4500	n/a	ajcdc@clark.net	n/a
Americans for Religious Liberty	Box 6656, Silver Spring, Maryland 20916	301-598-2447	301-438-8424	n/a	n/a
Americans United for Separation of Church and State	1816 Jefferson Place, N.W., Washington, D.C. 20036	202-466-3234	202-466-2587	amerunited@aol.com	http://www.au.org/
Anti-Defamation League	823 United Nations Plaza, New York, New York 10017	212-490-2525	212-867-0779	n/a	http://www.adl.org/
Baptists Joint Committee	200 Maryland Avenue, N.E. Washington, D.C. 20002-5797	202-544-4226	202-544-2094	bjc_intern@bjcpa.com	http://www.erols.com/bjcpa/
Church State Council	1228 N Street, Sacramento, California 95814	916-446-2552	916-446-6543	n/a	http://www.churchstate.org/

RELIGION AND THE LAW

ORGANIZATION	ADDRESS	TELEPHONE NUMBER	FAX NUMBER	E-MAIL	INTERNET WEBSITE
Freedom from Religion Foundation	P.O. Box 750, Madison, Wisconsin 53701	608-256-8900	608-256-1116	dbarker@mailbag.com	http://www.infi.org/ffrf/
The Fund for Constitutional Government	122 Maryland Avenue, N.E., Washington, D.C. 20002	202-546-3799	202-543-3156	FunConGov@aol.com	n/a
Individual Rights Foundation	Box 67398, Los Angeles, California 9006-9507	310-843-3699	310-843-3629	76042.3271@compuserve.com	n/a Institute for First Amendment Studies
The Interfaith Alliance	1012 14th Street N.W., Suite 700, Washington, D.C. 20005	202-639-6370	202-639-6375	mail@tialliance.org	http://www.tialliance.org/
National Committee for Amish Religious Freedom	30650 Six Mile Road, Livonia, Michigan 48154	734-427-1414	n/a	amish@holycrosslivonia.org	http://holycrosslivonia.org/amish/
National Committee for Public Education and Religious Liberty (PEARL)	165 East 56th Street, New York, New York 10022	212-750-6461	212-319-0975	doyle@tiac.net	http://www.tiac.net/users/doyle/PEARL.html
Pennsylvania Alliance for Democracy	P.O. Box 366, Harrisburg, Pennsylvania 17108-0366	1-800-944-7732	n/a	exposepa@libertynet.org	http://www.libertynet.org/exposepa/
People for the American Way	2000 M Street N.W., Suite 400, Washington, D.C. 20036	202-467-4999	202-293-2672	pfaw@pfaw.org	http://www.pfaw.org./

APPENDIX 2:
CHART OF SIGNIFICANT SUPREME COURT FIRST AMENDMENT DECISIONS INVOLVING RELIGION AND PUBLIC EDUCATION

CONSTITUTIONAL ISSUE	YEAR	CASE NAME	CITATION	DECISION
RELIGION IN PUBLIC SCHOOLS	1940	Minersville v. Gobitis	310 U.S. 586	A public school may require students to salute the flag and pledge allegiance even if it violates their religious scruples.
RELIGION IN PUBLIC SCHOOLS	1943	West Virginia State Board of Education v. Barnette	319 U.S. 624	Reversed "Minersville" — held that no one can be forced to salute the flag or say the pledge of allegiance if it violates the individual conscience.
RELIGION IN PUBLIC SCHOOLS	1948	McCollum v. Board of Education	333 U.S. 203	Religious instruction in public schools is unconstitutional because it violates the establishment clause.
RELIGION IN PUBLIC SCHOOLS	1952	Zorach v. Clausen	343 U.S. 306	Release time from public school for the purposes of religious instruction does not violate the establishment clause.
RELIGION IN PUBLIC SCHOOLS	1962	Engel v. Vitale	370 U.S. 421	School prayer ruled unconstitutional.
RELIGION IN PUBLIC SCHOOLS	1963	Abington School District v. Schempp	374 U.S. 203	Bible reading over school intercom is unconstitutional.

CONSTITUTIONAL ISSUE	YEAR	CASE NAME	CITATION	DECISION
RELIGION IN PUBLIC SCHOOLS	1963	Murray v. Curlett	374 U.S. 203	Requiring a child to participate in Bible reading and prayer is unconstitutional.
RELIGION IN PUBLIC SCHOOLS	1968	Epperson v. Arkansas	393 U.S. 97	The state cannot ban the teaching of evolution.
RELIGION IN PUBLIC SCHOOLS	1980	Stone v. Graham	449 U.S. 39	Posting of the Ten Commandments in schools is unconstitutional.
RELIGION IN PUBLIC SCHOOLS	1985	Wallace v. Jaffree	472 U.S. 38	State law enforcing a moment of silence in schools had a religious purpose and is therefore unconstitutional.
RELIGION IN PUBLIC SCHOOLS	1987	Edwards v. Aquillard	482 U.S. 578	State law requiring equal treatment for creationism has a religious purpose and is therefore unconstitutional.
RELIGION IN PUBLIC SCHOOLS	1990	Board of Education v. Mergens	496 U.S. 226	The Equal Access Act does not violate the First Amendment.
RELIGION IN PUBLIC SCHOOLS	1992	Lee v. Weisman	112 SCt. 2649	Prayer at public school graduation ceremonies violates the establishment clause and is therefore unconstitutional.
RELIGION IN PUBLIC SCHOOLS	1993	Lamb's Chapel et al. v. Center Moriches Union Free School District	___ U.S. ___	School districts cannot deny churches access to school premises after-hours

APPENDIX 2

CONSTITUTIONAL ISSUE	YEAR	CASE NAME	CITATION	DECISION
RELIGION IN STATE COLLEGES AND UNIVERSITIES	1981	Widmar v. Vincent	454 U.S. 263	A state university cannot refuse to grant a student religious group "equal access" to facilities that are open to other student groups.
RELIGION IN STATE COLLEGES AND UNIVERSITIES	1995	Rosenberger v. Rector and Visitors of the University of Virginia	___ U.S. ___	Student activity funds can be used to fund a Christian perspective student magazine called "Wide Awake."
RELIGIOUS SCHOOL SUPPORT	1947	Everson v. Board of Education	330 U.S. 1	State reimbursement for bus fares to attend religious schools is constitutional.
RELIGIOUS SCHOOL SUPPORT	1968	Board of Education v. Allen	392 U.S. 236	State's textbook loan program to private and religious schools is constitutional.
RELIGIOUS SCHOOL SUPPORT	1971	Lemon v. Kurtzman	403 U.S. 602	State supplements Catholic school teachers' salaries ruled unconstitutional.
RELIGIOUS SCHOOL SUPPORT	1971	Tilton v. Richardson	403 U.S. 671	Federal funding to private
RELIGIOUS SCHOOL SUPPORT	1973	Committee v. Nyquist	413 U.S. 756 (1973)	States cannot reimburse parents for sending their children to religious schools.
RELIGIOUS SCHOOL SUPPORT	1973	Sloan v. Lemon	413 U.S. 825	States cannot reimburse parents for sending their children to religious schools.

CONSTITUTIONAL ISSUE	YEAR	CASE NAME	CITATION	DECISION
RELIGIOUS SCHOOL SUPPORT	1975	Meek v. Pittenger	421 U.S. 349	States can lend textbooks to religious schools but no other materials.
RELIGIOUS SCHOOL SUPPORT	1976	Roemer v. Board of Public Works	426 U.S. 736	States can provide grants to private and religious colleges.
RELIGIOUS SCHOOL SUPPORT	1980	Committee for Public Education v. Regan	444 U.S. 646	States can reimburse religious schools for the cost of giving standardized tests.
RELIGIOUS SCHOOL SUPPORT	1983	Mueller v. Allen	463 U.S. 388	Taxpayers can deduct tuition
RELIGIOUS SCHOOL SUPPORT	1985	Aquilar v. Felton	473 U.S. 402	Sending public school teachers to religious schools to provide instruction is unconstitutional.
RELIGIOUS SCHOOL SUPPORT	1993	Zobrest et al. v. Catalina Foothills School District	___ U.S. ___	School district does not violate the Establishment Clause by furnishing a sign-interpreter to a deaf child in a sectarian school.
RELIGIOUS SCHOOL SUPPORT	1994	Kiryas Joel Village School District v. Grumet	___ U.S. ___	School district carved out for religious reasons and financed by public funds violates the Establishment Clause.

APPENDIX 2

CONSTITUTIONAL ISSUE	YEAR	CASE NAME	CITATION	DECISION
RELIGIOUS SCHOOL SUPPORT	1997	Agostini v. Felton	____ U.S. ____	Reversed "Aquilar" — held that public school teachers providing supplemental, remedial instruction to disadvantaged students in religious schools does not violate the establishment clause.

APPENDIX 3:

THE RELIGIOUS FREEDOM RESTORATION ACT OF 1993
(H.R. 1308)

SECTION 1. SHORT TITLE.

This Act may be cited as the 'Religious Freedom Restoration Act of 1993'.

SECTION 2. CONGRESSIONAL FINDINGS AND DECLARATION OF PURPOSES.

(a) Findings: The Congress finds that—

(1) the framers of the Constitution, recognizing free exercise of religion as an unalienable right, secured its protection in the First Amendment to the Constitution;

(2) laws 'neutral' toward religion may burden religious exercise as surely as laws intended to interfere with religious exercise;

(3) governments should not substantially burden religious exercise without compelling justification;

(4) in Employment Division v. Smith, 494 U.S. 872 (1990) the Supreme Court virtually eliminated the requirement that the government justify burdens on religious exercise imposed by laws neutral toward religion; and

(5) the compelling interest test as set forth in prior Federal court rulings is a workable test for striking sensible balances between religious liberty and competing prior governmental interests.

(b) Purposes: The purposes of this Act are—

(1) to restore the compelling interest test as set forth in Sherbert v. Verner, 374 U.S. 398 (1963) and Wisconsin v. Yoder, 406 U.S. 205 (1972) and to guarantee its application in all cases where free exercise of religion is substantially burdened; and

(2) to provide a claim or defense to persons whose religious exercise is substantially burdened by government.

SECTION 3. FREE EXERCISE OF RELIGION PROTECTED.

(a) In General: Government shall not substantially burden a person's exercise of religion even if the burden results from a rule of general applicability, except as provided in subsection (b).

(b) Exception: Government may substantially burden a person's exercise of religion only if it demonstrates that application of the burden to the person—

(1) is in furtherance of a compelling governmental interest; and

(2) is the least restrictive means of furthering that compelling governmental interest.

(c) Judicial Relief: A person whose religious exercise has been burdened in violation of this section may assert that violation as a claim or defense in a judicial proceeding and obtain appropriate relief against a government. Standing to assert a claim or defense under this section shall be governed by the general rules of standing under article III of the Constitution.

SECTION 4. ATTORNEYS FEES.

(a) Judicial Proceedings: Section 722 of the Revised Statutes (42 U.S.C. 1988) is amended by inserting 'the Religious Freedom Restoration Act of 1993,' before 'or title VI of the Civil Rights Act of 1964'.

(b) Administrative Proceedings: Section 504(b)(1)(C) of title 5, United States Code, is amended—

(1) by striking 'and' at the end of clause (ii);

(2) by striking the semicolon at the end of clause (iii) and inserting ', and'; and

(3) by inserting '(iv) the Religious Freedom Restoration Act of 1993;' after clause (iii).

SECTION 5. DEFINITIONS.

As used in this Act —

(1) the term 'government' includes a branch, department, agency, instrumentality, and official (or other person acting under color of law) of the United States, a State, or a subdivision of a State;

(2) the term 'State' includes the District of Columbia, the Commonwealth of Puerto Rico, and each territory and possession of the United States;

(3) the term 'demonstrates' means meets the burdens of going forward with the evidence and of persuasion; and

(4) the term 'exercise of religion' means the exercise of religion under the First Amendment to the Constitution.

SECTION 6. APPLICABILITY.

(a) In General.—This Act applies to all Federal and State law, and the implementation of that law, whether statutory or otherwise, and whether adopted before or after the enactment of this Act .

(b) Rule of Construction.—Federal statutory law adopted after the date of the enactment of this Act is subject to this Act unless such law explicitly excludes such application by reference to this Act .

(c) Religious Belief Unaffected.—Nothing in this Act shall be construed to authorize any government to burden any religious belief.

SECTION 7. ESTABLISHMENT CLAUSE UNAFFECTED.

Nothing in this Act shall be construed to affect, interpret, or in any way address that portion of the First Amendment prohibiting laws respecting the establishment of religion (referred to in this section as the 'Establishment Clause'). Granting government funding, benefits, or exemptions, to the extent permissible under the Establishment Clause, shall not constitute a violation of this Act. As used in this section, the term 'granting', used with respect to government funding, benefits, or exemptions, does not include the denial of government funding, benefits, or exemptions.

APPENDIX 4:

FEDERAL GUIDELINES ON RELIGIOUS EXERCISE AND EXPRESSION IN THE FEDERAL WORKPLACE

Section 1. Guidelines for Religious Exercise and Religious Expression in the Federal Workplace

Executive departments and agencies ("agencies") shall permit personal religious expression by federal employees to the greatest extent possible, consistent with requirements of law and interests in workplace efficiency as described in this set of guidelines. Agencies shall not discriminate against employees on the basis of religion, require religious participation or non-participation as a condition of employment, or permit religious harassment. And agencies shall accommodate employees' exercise of their religion in the circumstances specified in these guidelines. These requirements are but applications of the general principle that agencies shall treat all employees with the same respect and consideration, regardless of their religion, or lack thereof.

A. Religious Expression

As a matter of law, agencies shall not restrict personal religious expression by employees in the federal workplace except where the employee's interest in the expression is outweighed by the government's interest in the efficient provision of public services or where the expression intrudes upon the legitimate rights of other employees or creates the appearance, to a reasonable observer, of an official endorsement of religion. The examples cited in these guidelines as permissible forms of religious expression will rarely, if ever, fall within these exceptions.

As a general rule, agencies may not regulate employees' personal religious expression on the basis of its content or viewpoint. In other words, agencies generally may not suppress employees' private religious speech in the workplace while leaving unregulated other private employee speech that has a comparable effect on the efficiency of the workplace—including ideological speech on politics and other topics—because to do so would be to engage in presumptively unlawful content or viewpoint discrimination.

Agencies, however, may, in their discretion, reasonably regulate the time, place and manner of all employee speech, provided such regulations do not discriminate on the basis of content or viewpoint.

The federal government generally has the authority to regulate an employee's private speech, including religious speech, where the employee's interest in that speech is outweighed by the government's interest in promoting the efficiency of the public services it performs. Agencies should exercise this authority evenhandedly and with restraint, and with regard for the fact that Americans are used to expressions of disagreement on controversial subjects, including religious ones.

Agencies are not required, however, to permit employees to use work time to pursue religious or ideological agendas. Federal employees are paid to perform official work, not to engage in personal religious or ideological campaigns during work hours.

(1) Expression in Private Work Areas

Employees should be permitted to engage in private religious expression in personal work areas not regularly open to the public to the same extent that they may engage in non- religious private expression, subject to reasonable content- and viewpoint-neutral standards and restrictions: Such religious expression must be permitted so long as it does not interfere with the agency's carrying out of its official responsibilities.

(2) Expression among Fellow Employees

Employees should be permitted to engage in religious expression with fellow employees, to the same extent that they may engage in comparable non-religious private expression, subject to reasonable and content-neutral standards and restrictions.

Such expression should not be restricted so long as it does not interfere with workplace efficiency. Though agencies are entitled to regulate such employee speech based on reasonable predictions of disruption, they should not restrict speech based on merely hypothetical concerns, having little basis in fact, that the speech will have a deleterious effect on workplace efficiency.

(3) Expression Directed at Fellow Employees

Employees are permitted to engage in religious expression directed at fellow employees, and may even attempt to persuade fellow employees of the correctness of their religious views to the same extent as those employees may engage in comparable speech not involving religion. Some religions encourage adherents to spread the faith at every opportunity, a duty that can encompass the adherent's workplace. As a general matter, proselytizing is as entitled to constitutional protection as any other form of speech—as long as a reasonable observer would not interpret the expression as government endorsement of religion.

Employees may urge a colleague to participate or not to participate in religious activities to the same extent that, consistent with concerns of workplace efficiency, they may urge their colleagues to engage in or refrain from other personal endeavors. But employees must refrain from such expression when a fellow employee asks that it stop or otherwise demonstrates that it is unwelcome. Such expression by supervisors is subject to special consideration as discussed in Section B(2) of these guidelines.

(4) Expression in Areas Accessible to the Public

Where the public has access to the federal workplace, all federal employers must be sensitive to the Establishment Clause's requirement that expression not create the reasonable impression that the government is sponsoring, endorsing, or inhibiting religion generally, or favoring or disfavoring a particular religion. This is particularly important in agencies with adjudicatory functions.

However, even in workplaces open to the public, not all private employee religious expression is forbidden. For example, federal employees may wear personal religious jewelry absent special circumstances, such as safety concerns, that might require a ban on all similar non-religious jewelry.

Employees may also display religious art and literature in their personal work areas to the same extent that they may display other art and literature, so long as the viewing public would reasonably understand the religious expression to be that of the employee acting in her personal capacity, and not that of the government itself.

Similarly, in their private time employees may discuss religion with willing coworkers in public spaces to the same extent as they may discuss other subjects, so long as the public would reasonably understand the religious expression to be that of the employees acting in their personal capacities.

B. Religious Discrimination

Federal agencies may not discriminate against employees on the basis of their religion, religious beliefs, or views concerning religion.

(1) Discrimination in Terms and Conditions

No agency within the executive branch may promote, refuse to promote, hire, refuse to hire, or otherwise favor or disfavor, an employee or potential employee because of his or her religion, religious beliefs, or views concerning religion.

(2) Coercion of Employee's Participation or Nonparticipation in Religious Activities

A person holding supervisory authority over an employee may not, explicitly or implicitly, insist that the employee participate in religious activities as a condition of continued employment, promotion, salary increases, preferred job assignments, or any other incidents of employment. Nor may a supervisor insist that an employee refrain from participating in religious activities outside the workplace except pursuant to otherwise legal, neutral restrictions that apply to employees' off-duty conduct and expression in general (e.g., restrictions on political activities prohibited by the Hatch Act).

This prohibition leaves supervisors free to engage in some kinds of speech about religion. Where a supervisor's religious expression is not coercive and is understood as his or her personal view, that expression is protected in the federal workplace in the same way and to the same extent as other constitutionally valued speech. For example, if surrounding circumstances indicate that the expression is merely the personal view of the supervisor and that employees are free to reject or ignore the supervisor's point of view or invitation without any harm to their careers or professional lives, such expression is so protected.

Because supervisors have the power to hire, fire, or promote, employees may reasonably perceive their supervisors' religious expression as coercive, even if it was not intended as such. Therefore, supervisors should be careful to ensure that their statements and actions are such that employees do not perceive any coercion of religious or non-religious behavior (or respond as if such coercion is occurring), and should, where necessary, take appropriate steps to dispel such misperceptions.

(3) Hostile Work Environment and Harassment

The law against workplace discrimination protects federal employees from being subjected to a hostile environment, or religious harassment, in the form of religiously discriminatory intimidation, or pervasive or severe religious ridicule or insult, whether by supervisors or fellow workers. Whether particular conduct gives rise to a hostile environment, or constitutes impermissible religious harassment, will usually depend upon its frequency or repetitiveness, as well as its severity. The use of derogatory language in an assaultive manner can constitute statutory religious harassment if it is severe or invoked repeatedly. A single incident, if sufficiently abusive, might also constitute statutory harassment.

However, although employees should always be guided by general principles of civility and workplace efficiency, a hostile environment is not created by the bare expression of speech with which some employees might disagree. In a country where freedom of speech and religion are guaranteed, citizens should expect to be exposed to ideas with which they disagree.

C. Accommodation of Religious Exercise

Federal law requires an agency to accommodate employees' exercise of their religion unless such accommodation would impose an undue hardship on the conduct of the agency's operations. Though an agency need not make an accommodation that will result in more than a *de minimis* cost to the agency, that cost or hardship nevertheless must be real rather than speculative or hypothetical: The accommodation should be made unless it would cause an actual cost to the agency or to other employees or an actual disruption of work, or unless it is otherwise barred by law.

In addition, religious accommodation cannot be disfavored vis-á-vis other, non-religious accommodations. Therefore, a religious accommodation cannot be denied if the agency regularly permits similar accommodations for non-religious purposes.

In those cases where an agency's work rule imposes a substantial burden on a particular employee's exercise of religion, the agency must go further: An agency should grant the employee an exemption from that rule, unless the agency has a compelling interest in denying the exemption and there is no less restrictive means of furthering that interest.

D. Establishment of Religion

Supervisors and employees must not engage in activities or expression that a reasonable observer would interpret as government endorsement or denigration of religion or a particular religion. Activities of employees need not be officially sanctioned in order to violate this principle; if, in all the circumstances, the activities would leave a reasonable observer with the impression that government was endorsing, sponsoring, or inhibiting religion generally or favoring or disfavoring a particular religion, they are not permissible. Diverse factors, such as the context of the expression or whether official channels of communication are used are relevant to what a reasonable observer would conclude.

Section 2. Guiding Legal Principles

In applying the guidance set forth in Section 1 of this order, executive branch departments and agencies should consider the following legal principles.

A. Religious Expression.

It is well-established that the Free Speech Clause of the First Amendment protects government employees in the workplace. This right encompasses a right to speak about religious subjects. The Free Speech Clause also prohibits the government from singling out religious expression for disfavored treatment: "[P]rivate religious speech, far from being a First Amendment orphan, is a fully protected under the Free Speech Clause as secular private expression," *Capitol Sq. Review Bd. v. Pinette*, 115 S. Ct. 2448 (1995).

Accordingly, in the government workplace, employee religious expression cannot be regulated because of its religious character, and such religious speech typically cannot be singled out for harsher treatment that other comparable expression.

Many religions strongly encourage their adherents to spread the faith by persuasion and example at every opportunity, a duty that can extend to the adherents' workplace. As a general matter, proselytizing is entitled to the same constitutional protection as any other form of speech. Therefore, in the governmental workplace, proselytizing should not be singled out because of its content for harsher treatment than non-religious expression.

However, it is also well-established that the government in its role as employer has broader discretion to regulate its employees speech in the workplace than it does to regulate speech among the public at large. Employees' expression on matters of public concern can be regulated if the employees' interest in the speech is outweighed by the interest of the government, as an employer, in promoting the efficiency of the public services it performs through its employees.

Governmental employers also possess substantial discretion to impose content-neutral and viewpoint-neutral time, place, and manner rules regulating private employee expression in the workplace, though they may not structure or administer such rules to discriminate against particular viewpoints.

Furthermore, employee speech can be regulated or discouraged if it impairs discipline by superiors, has a detrimental impact on close working relationships for which personal loyalty and confidence are necessary, impedes the performance of the speaker's duties or interferes with the regular operation of the enterprise, or demonstrates that the employee holds views that could lead his employer or the public reasonably to question whether he can perform his duties adequately.

Consistent with its fully protected character, employee religious speech should be treated, within the federal workplace, like other expression on issues of public concern: In a particular case, an employer can discipline an employee for engaging in speech if the value of the speech is outweighed by the employer's interest in promoting the efficiency of the public services it performs through its employee.

Typically, however, the religious speech cited as permissible in the various examples included in these guidelines will not unduly impede these interests and should not be regulated. And rules regulating employee speech, like other rules regulating speech, must be carefully drawn to avoid any unnecessary limiting or chilling of protected speech.

B. Discrimination in Terms and Conditions.

Title VII of the Civil Rights Act of 1964 makes it unlawful for employers, both private and public, to "fail or refuse to hire or to discharge any individual or otherwise to discriminate against any individual with respect to compensation, terms, conditions, or privileges of employment, because of such individual's ... religion." 42 U.S.C. § 2000e-2(a)(1).

The federal government also is bound by the equal protection component of the Due Process Clause of the Fifth Amendment, which bars intentional discrimination on the basis of religion. Moreover, the prohibition on religious discrimination in employment applies with particular force to the federal government, for Article VI, clause 3 of the Constitution bars the government from enforcing any religious test as a requirement for qualification to any office. In addition, if a government law, regulation or practice facially discriminates against employees' private exercise of religion or is intended to infringe upon or restrict private religious exercise, then that law, regulation, or practice implicates the Free Exercise Clause of the First Amendment.

Last, under the Religious Freedom Restoration Act, 42 U.S.C. § 2000bb-1, federal governmental action that substantially burdens a private party's exercise of religion can be enforced only if it is justified by a compelling interest and is narrowly tailored to advance that interest. [Note: The Religious Freedom Restoration Act has since been declared unconstitutional by the Supreme Court.]

C. Coercion of Employees' Participation or Nonparticipation in Religious Activities

The ban on religious discrimination is broader than simply guaranteeing nondiscriminatory treatment in formal employment decisions such as hiring and promotion. It applies to all terms and conditions of employment. It follows that the federal government may not require or coerce its employees to engage in religious activities or to refrain from engaging in religious activity. For example, a supervisor may not demand attendance at (or a refusal to attend) religious services as a condition of continued employment or promotion, or as a criterion affecting assignment of job duties.

Quid pro quo discrimination of this sort is illegal. Indeed, wholly apart from the legal prohibitions against coercion, supervisors may not insist upon employees' conformity to religious behavior in their private lives any more than they can insist on conformity to any other private conduct unrelated to employees' ability to carry out their duties.

D. Hostile Work Environment and Harassment

Employers violate Title VII's ban on discrimination by creating or tolerating a "hostile environment" in which an employee is subject to discriminatory intimidation, ridicule, or insult sufficiently severe or pervasive to alter the conditions of the victim's employment. This statutory standard can be triggered (at the very least) when an employee, because of her or his religion or lack thereof, is exposed to intimidation, ridicule, and insult.

The hostile conduct—which may take the form of speech—need not come from supervisors or from the employer. Fellow employees can create a hostile environment through their own words and actions.

The existence of some offensive workplace conduct does not necessarily constitute harassment under Title VII. Occasional and isolated utterances of an epithet that engenders offensive feelings in an employee typically would not affect conditions of employment, and therefore would not in and of itself constitute harassment. A hostile environment, for Title VII purposes, is not created by the bare expression of speech with which one disagrees.

For religious harassment to be illegal under Title VII, it must be sufficiently severe or pervasive to alter the conditions of employment and create an abusive working environment. Whether conduct can be the predicate for a finding of religious harassment under Title VII depends on the totality of the circumstances, such as the nature of the verbal or physical conduct at issue and the context in which the alleged incidents occurred.

As the Supreme Court has said in an analogous context:

"[W]hether an environment is hostile' or abusive' can be determined only by looking at all the circumstances. These may include the frequency of the discriminatory conduct; its severity; whether it is physically threatening or humiliating, or a mere offensive utterance; and whether it unreasonably interferes with an employee's work performance. The effect on the employee's psychological well-being is, of course, relevant to determining whether the plaintiff actually found the environment abusive." *Harris v. Forklift Systems Inc.*, 510 U.S. 17, 23 (1993).

The use of derogatory language directed at an employee can rise to the level of religious harassment if it is severe or invoked repeatedly. In particular, repeated religious slurs and negative religious stereotypes, or continued disparagement of an employee's religion or ritual practices, or lack thereof, can constitute harassment. It is not necessary that the harassment be explicitly religious in character or that the slurs reference religion: It is sufficient that the harassment is directed at an employee because of the employee's religion or lack thereof.

That is to say, Title VII can be violated by employer tolerance of repeated slurs, insults and/or abuse not explicitly religious in nature if that conduct would not have occurred but for the targeted employee's religious belief or lack of religious belief.

Finally, although proselytization directed at fellow employees is generally permissible, subject to the special considerations relating to supervisor expression discussed elsewhere in these guidelines, such activity must stop if the listener asks that it stops or otherwise demonstrates that it is unwelcome.

E. Accommodation of Religious Exercise

Title VII requires employers "to reasonably accommodate...an employee's or prospective employee's religious observance or practice" unless such accommodation would impose an "undue hardship on the conduct of the employer's business." 42 U.S.C. § 2000e(j). For example, by statute, if an employee's religious beliefs require her to be absent from work, the federal government must grant that employee compensation time for overtime work, to be applied against the time lost, unless to do so would harm the ability of the agency to carry out its mission efficiently. 5 U.S.C. § 5550a.

Though an employer need not incur more than de minimis costs in providing an accommodation, the employer hardship nevertheless must be real rather than speculative or hypothetical. Religious accommodation cannot be disfavored relative to other, non-religious, accommodations.

If an employer regularly permits accommodations for non-religious purposes, it cannot deny comparable religious accommodation: "Such an arrangement would display a discrimination against religious practices that is the antithesis of reasonableness." *Ansonia Bd. of Educ. v. Philbrook*, 479 U.S. 60, 71 (1986).

In the federal government workplace, if neutral workplace rules—that is, rules that do not single out religious or religiously motivated conduct for disparate treatment—impose a substantial burden on a particular employee's exercise of religion, the Religious Freedom Restoration Act requires the employer to grant the employee an exemption from that neutral rule, unless the employer has a compelling interest in denying an exemption and there is no less restrictive means of furthering that interest. 42 U.S.C. § 2000bb-1. [Note: The Religious Freedom Restoration Act has since been declared unconstitutional by the Supreme Court.]

F. Establishment of Religion.

The Establishment Clause of the First Amendment prohibits the government—including its employees—from acting in a manner that would lead a reasonable observer to conclude that the government is sponsoring, endorsing, or inhibiting religion generally or favoring or disfavoring a particular religion.

For example, where the public has access to the federal workplace, employee religious expression should be prohibited where the public reasonably would perceive that the employee is acting in an official, rather than a private, capacity, or under circumstances that would lead a reasonable observer to conclude that the government is endorsing or disparaging religion.

The Establishment Clause also forbids federal employees from using government funds or resources (other than those facilities generally available to government employees) for private religious use.

Section 3. General

These guidelines shall govern the internal management of the civilian executive branch. They are not intended to create any new right, benefit, or trust responsibility, substantive or procedural, enforceable at law or equity by a party against the United States, its agencies, its officers, or any person. Questions regarding interpretation of these guidelines should be brought to the Office of the General Counsel or Legal Counsel in each department and agency.

APPENDIX 5:

PRESIDENTIAL DIRECTIVE ON RELIGIOUS EXPRESSION IN PUBLIC SCHOOLS, JULY 13, 1995

Religious freedom is perhaps the most precious of all American liberties—called by many our "first freedom." Many of the first European settlers in North America sought refuge from religious persecution in their native countries. Since that time, people of faith and religious institutions have played a central role in the history of this Nation.

In the First Amendment, our Bill of Rights recognizes the twin pillars of religious liberty: the constitutional protection for the free exercise of religion, and the constitutional prohibition of the establishment of religion by the state. Our Nation's founders knew that religion helps to give our people the character without which a democracy cannot survive. Our founders also recognized the need for a space of freedom between government and the people—that the government must not be permitted to coerce the conscience of any individual or group.

In the over 200 years since the First Amendment was included in our Constitution, religion and religious institutions have thrived throughout the United States. In 1993, I was proud to reaffirm the historic place of religion when I signed the Religious Freedom Restoration Act, which restores a high legal standard to protect the exercise of religion from being inappropriately burdened by government action.

In the greatest traditions of American citizenship, a broad coalition of individuals and organizations came together to support the fullest protection for religious practice and expression.

RELIGIOUS EXPRESSION IN PUBLIC SCHOOLS

I share the concern and frustration that many Americans feel about situations where the protections accorded by the First Amendment are not recognized or understood. This problem has manifested itself in our Nation's public schools. It appears that some school officials, teachers and parents have assumed that religious expression of any type is either inappropriate, or forbidden altogether, in public schools.

As our courts have reaffirmed, however, nothing in the First Amendment converts our public schools into religion-free zones, or requires all religious expression to be left behind at the schoolhouse door. While the government may not use schools to coerce the consciences of our students, or to convey official endorsement of religion, the government's schools also may not discriminate against private religious expression during the school day.

I have been advised by the Department of Justice and the Department of Education that the First Amendment permits—and protects—a greater degree of religious expression in public schools than many Americans may now understand. The Departments of Justice and Education have advised me that, while application may depend upon specific factual contexts and will require careful consideration in particular cases, the following principles are among those that apply to religious expression in our schools:

Student Prayer and Religious Discussion

The Establishment Clause of the First Amendment does not prohibit purely private religious speech by students. Students therefore have the same right to engage in individual or group prayer and religious discussion during the school day as they do to engage in other comparable activity.

For example, students may read their Bibles or other scriptures, say grace before meals, and pray before tests to the same extent they may engage in comparable non-disruptive activities. Local school authorities possess substantial discretion to impose rules of order and other pedagogical restrictions on student activities, but they may not structure or administer such rules to discriminate against religious activity or speech.

Generally, students may pray in a nondisruptive manner when not engaged in school activities or instruction, and subject to the rules that normally pertain in the applicable setting. Specifically, students in informal settings, such as cafeterias and hallways, may pray and discuss their religious views with each other, subject to the same rules of order as apply to other student activities and speech. Students may also speak to, and attempt to persuade, their peers about religious topics just as they do with regard to political topics. School officials, however, should intercede to stop student speech that constitutes harassment aimed at a student or a group of students.

Students may also participate in before or after school events with religious content, such as "see you at the flag pole" gatherings, on the same terms as they may participate in other noncurriculum activities on school premises. School officials may neither discourage nor encourage participation in such an event.

The right to engage in voluntary prayer or religious discussion free from discrimination does not include the right to have a captive audience to listen, or to compel other students to participate. Teachers and school administrators should ensure that no student is in any way coerced to participate in religious activity.

Graduation Prayer and Baccalaureates

Under current Supreme Court decisions, school officials may not mandate or organize prayer at graduation, nor organize religious baccalaureate ceremonies. If a school generally opens its facilities to private groups, it must make its facilities available on the same terms to organizers of privately sponsored religious baccalaureate services. A school may not extend preferential treatment to baccalaureate ceremonies and may in some instances be obliged to disclaim official endorsement of such ceremonies.

Official Neutrality Regarding Religious Activity

Teachers and school administrators, when acting in those capacities, are representatives of the state and are prohibited by the establishment clause from soliciting or encouraging religious activity, and from participating in such activity with students. Teachers and administrators also are prohibited from discouraging activity because of its religious content, and from soliciting or encouraging antireligious activity.

Teaching About Religion

Public schools may not provide religious instruction, but they may teach about religion, including the Bible or other scripture: the history of religion, comparative religion, the Bible—or other scripture—as literature, and the role of religion in the history of the United States and other countries all are permissible public school subjects.

Similarly, it is permissible to consider religious influences on art, music, literature, and social studies. Although public schools may teach about religious holidays, including their religious aspects, and may celebrate the secular aspects of holidays, schools may not observe holidays as religious events or promote such observance by students.

Student Assignments

Students may express their beliefs about religion in the form of homework, artwork, and other written and oral assignments free of discrimination based on the religious content of their submissions. Such home and classroom work should be judged by ordinary academic standards of substance and relevance, and against other legitimate pedagogical concerns identified by the school.

Religious Literature

Students have a right to distribute religious literature to their schoolmates on the same terms as they are permitted to distribute other literature that is unrelated to school curriculum or activities. Schools may impose the same reasonable time, place, and manner or other constitutional restrictions on distribution of religious literature as they do on nonschool literature generally, but they may not single out religious literature for special regulation.

Religious Excusals

Subject to applicable State laws, schools enjoy substantial discretion to excuse individual students from lessons that are objectionable to the student or students' parents on religious or other conscientious grounds. School officials may neither encourage or discourage students from availing themselves of an excusal option. Under the Religious Freedom Restoration Act, if it is proved that particular lessons substantially burden a student's free exercise of religion and if school cannot prove a compelling interest in requiring attendance, the school would be legally required to excuse the student.

Released Time

Subject to applicable State laws, schools have the discretion to dismiss students to off-premises religious instruction, provided that schools do not encourage or discourage participation or penalize those who do not attend. Schools may not allow religious instruction by outsiders on school premises during the school day.

Teaching Values

Though schools must be neutral with respect to religion, they may play an active role with respect to teaching civic values and virtue, and the moral code that holds us together as a community. The fact that some of these values are held also by religions does not make it unlawful to teach them in school.

Student Garb

Students may display religious messages on items of clothing to the same extent that they are permitted to display other comparable messages. Religious messages may not be singled out for suppression, but rather are subject to the same rules as generally apply to comparable messages. When wearing particular attire, such as yarmulkes and head scarves, during the school day is part of students' religious practice, under the Religious Freedom Restoration Act, schools generally may not prohibit the wearing of such items.

I hereby direct the Secretary of Education, in consultation with the Attorney General, to use appropriate means to ensure that public school districts and school officials in the United States are informed, by the start of the coming school year, of the principles set forth above.

THE EQUAL ACCESS ACT

The Equal Access Act is designed to ensure that, consistent with the First Amendment, student religious activities are accorded the same access to public school facilities as are student secular activities.

Based on decisions of the Federal courts, as well as its interpretations of the Act, the Department of Justice has advised me of its position that the Act should be interpreted as providing, among other things, that:

General Provisions

Student religious groups at public secondary schools have the same right of access to school facilities as is enjoyed by other comparable student groups. Under the Equal Access Act, a school receiving Federal funds that allows one or more student noncurriculum-related clubs to meet on its premises during noninstructional time may not refuse access to student religious groups.

Prayer Services and Worship Exercises Covered

A meeting, as defined and protected by the Equal Access Act, may include a prayer service, Bible reading, or other worship exercise.

Equal Access to Means of Publicizing Meetings

A school receiving Federal funds must allow student groups meeting under the Act to use the school media—including the public address system, the school newspaper, and the school bulletin board—to announce their meetings on the same terms as other noncurriculum-related student groups are allowed to use the school media. Any policy concerning the use of school media must be applied to all noncurriculum-related student groups in a nondiscriminatory matter. Schools, however, may inform students that certain groups are not school sponsored.

Lunchtime and Recess Covered

A school creates a limited open forum under the Equal Access Act, triggering equal access rights for religious groups, when it allows students to meet during their lunch periods or other noninstructional time during the school day, as well as when it allows students to meet before and after the school day.

I hereby direct the Secretary of Education, in consultation with the Attorney General, to use appropriate means to ensure that public school districts and school officials in the United States are informed, by the start of the coming school year, of these interpretations of the Equal Access Act.

APPENDIX 6:

SAMPLE SCHOOL DISTRICT POLICY ON RELIGIOUS ISSUES —WICOMICO COUNTY BOARD OF EDUCATION, SALISBURY, MARYLAND

PREAMBLE

Any discussion of the place of religion in public education must be grounded in the principle of freedom of conscience, particularly as it is embodied in this nation's First Amendment to the Constitution which states that "Congress shall make no law respecting an establishment of religion, or prohibiting the free exercise thereof . . . "

This inalienable right to religious liberty depends neither upon political authority nor upon any election but is rooted in the inviolable dignity of each person.

Teaching about religion, then, must adhere to the American experiment which cherishes beliefs that are a matter of conviction rather than coercion. It must foster learning in an atmosphere permeated by the values adopted by the Wicomico County school system: compassion, courtesy, freedom of thought and action, honesty, loyalty, respect for others' rights, responsibility, responsible citizenship, self-respect and tolerance.

While the Supreme Court has prohibited religious indoctrination by the public schools, the court has made clear that teaching about religion is permissible under the First Amendment. Operating under the principle that knowledge is preferable to ignorance and recognizing the significant role religion has played in this nation's public life and culture and in the wider arena of world history, the board supports teaching about religious history and tradition where appropriate in the curriculum.

POLICY

The board of education endorses teaching about religion where the curriculum guides indicate it is appropriate and when the classroom atmosphere encourages both teachers and students to be responsible and to respect the rights of each person. Such teaching must foster knowledge about religion, not indoctrination into religion; it should be academic, not devotional or testimonial; it should promote awareness of religion, not sponsor its practice; it should inform students about the diversity of religious views rather than impose one particular view; and it should promote understanding and respect rather than divisiveness.

Consequently, the board endorses, where appropriate and feasible, the professional development of teachers who wish to learn more about the constitutionally appropriate place of religion in the curriculum. The board also supports the development of new instructional materials that will reflect age-appropriate content and activities for teaching about religion.

GUIDELINES

To help school administrators and teachers interpret and apply the Wicomico County Board of Education policy regarding teaching about religion in the schools, the following guidelines have been developed by the Values Committee of the Wicomico County Board of Education in consultation with the First Liberty Institute.

PART 1: CURRICULUM

A. Religious instruction is the responsibility of parents and religious institutions, but teaching about religion is a legitimate part of a complete education on the elementary and secondary levels.

B. Teaching about religion should always operate within the context of First Amendment rights and responsibilities. In order to ensure the activity is constitutional, its purpose and effort should be to educate about rather than promote religion. The activity should also avoid excessive entanglement between the schools and religious organizations.

C. As a part of the curriculum, religious literature, music, drama and the arts may be included, provided each is intrinsic to the learning experience in the various fields of study and is presented objectively. Also, as part of the curriculum, students may be asked to read selections from sacred writings for their literary and historical qualities, but not for devotional purposes.

PART 2: SCHOOL PROGRAMS AND HOLIDAYS

A. School programs, performances and celebrations will serve an educational purpose. The inclusion of religious music, symbols, art or writings may be permitted if the religious content has an independent educational purpose which contributes to the stated objectives of the approved curriculum.

B. The use of religious symbols, provided they are used only as an example of cultural and religious heritage, is permitted as a teaching aid or resource. These symbols may be displayed only for the length of time that the instructional activity requires.

C. The Supreme Court has made clear that public schools may not sponsor religious celebrations but may teach about religion. Secular and religious holidays provide opportunities for educating students about history and cultures, as well as traditions of particular religious groups within a pluralistic society.

However, teachers must exercise special caution and sensitivity whenever discussion about religious holidays occurs. Presentation of materials dealing with religious holidays must be accurate, informed and descriptive. Focus should be on the origins, history and generally agreed-upon meanings of the holidays.

Since teachers will need to be aware of the diversity of religious beliefs in their classroom and in the county at large, they will need to be particularly sensitive to the rights of religious minorities as well as those who hold no religious belief. Respect for religious diversity in the classroom requires that teachers be fair and balanced in their treatment of religious holidays.

Teachers may not use the study of religious holidays as an opportunity to proselytize or to inject religious beliefs into the discussions. Teachers can teach through attribution, i.e., by reporting that "some Buddhists believe . . . "

D. On the elementary level, natural opportunities arise for discussion of religious holidays while studying different cultures and communities; in the secondary level, students of world history or literature will have opportunities to consider the holy days of religious traditions.

E. Teachers need to be aware of the major religious holidays of all the represented religions in their classrooms so as to avoid, as much as possible, creating an undue burden on students who choose not to attend school on those days.

PART 3: SCHEDULING

A. School scheduling should reasonably accommodate religious observances in the community. The yearly school calendar should minimize conflicts with the religious holidays of all faiths.

B. The Wicomico School calendar shall continue to recognize national, state, school and community observances. Special days beyond those specified on the calendar may be accommodated as reasonably as possible, with students being asked to make up assignments or examinations without loss of status or penalty.

PART 4: PROCEDURES

A. Recognizing the importance of religious liberty and freedom of conscience, school administrators and teachers will allow students to be excused, where it is feasible, from activities that are contrary to religious beliefs. Students are responsible for notifying school officials in advance and arranging for make-up work.

Students and/or staff members wishing to be excused from activities that are contrary to their religious beliefs may make that request of the appropriate teacher or supervisor, within a reasonable time period to allow accommodations to be made.

B. This policy holds for all lectures, programs and performances presented within the school during normal school hours. It is the responsibility of teachers and school officials to notify, whenever relevant, outside speakers and performers of Wicomico County's policy and its guidelines.

C. Disciplinary questions that relate to violations of this policy by teachers or administrators will be resolved through the already established procedures of the board.

D. Recognizing that no guidelines can give exhaustive treatment of this issue, the Superintendent may choose to refer disputes about implementation of this policy to an appropriate committee.[1]

---

[1] Source: The Freedom Forum First Amendment Center at Vanderbilt University.

APPENDIX 7:

STATEMENT OF FIRST PRINCIPLES

In the spirit of the First Amendment, we propose the following principles as civic ground rules for addressing conflicts in public education:

I. RELIGIOUS LIBERTY FOR ALL

Religious liberty is an inalienable right of every person. As Americans, we all share the responsibility to guard that right for every citizen. The Constitution of the United States with its Bill of Rights provides a civic framework of rights and responsibilities that enables Americans to work together for the common good in public education.

II. THE MEANING OF CITIZENSHIP

Citizenship in a diverse society means living with our deepest differences and committing ourselves to work for public policies that are in the best interest of all individuals, families, communities and our nation. The framers of our Constitution referred to this concept of moral responsibility as civic virtue.

III. PUBLIC SCHOOLS BELONG TO ALL CITIZENS

Public schools must model the democratic process and constitutional principles in the development of policies and curricula. Policy decisions by officials or governing bodies should be made only after appropriate involvement of those affected by the decision and with due consideration for the rights of those holding dissenting views.

IV. RELIGIOUS LIBERTY AND PUBLIC SCHOOLS

Public schools may not inculcate nor inhibit religion. They must be places where religion and religious conviction are treated with fairness and respect. Public schools uphold the First Amendment when they protect the religious liberty rights of students of all faiths or none. Schools demonstrate fairness when they ensure that the curriculum includes study about religion, where appropriate, as an important part of a complete education.

V. THE RELATIONSHIP BETWEEN PARENTS AND SCHOOLS FOR ALL

Parents are recognized as having the primary responsibility for the upbringing of their children, including education. Parents who send their children to public schools delegate to public school educators some of the responsibility for their children's education. In so doing, parents acknowledge the crucial role of educators without abdicating their parental duty. Parents may also choose not to send their children to public schools and have their children educated at home or in private schools. However, private citizens, including business leaders and others, also have the right to expect public education to give students tools for living in a productive democratic society. All citizens must have a shared commitment to offer students the best possible education. Parents have a special responsibility to participate in the activity of their children's schools. Children and schools benefit greatly when parents and educators work closely together to shape school policies and practices and to ensure that public education supports the societal values of their community without undermining family values and convictions.

VI. CONDUCT OF PUBLIC DISPUTES

Civil debate, the cornerstone of a true democracy, is vital to the success of any effort to improve and reform America's public schools. Personal attacks, name-calling, ridicule, and similar tactics destroy the fabric of our society and undermine the educational mission of our schools. Even when our differences are deep, all parties engaged in public disputes should treat one another with civility and respect, and should strive to be accurate and fair. Through constructive dialogue we have much to learn from one another.

APPENDIX 8:

DIRECTORY OF SPONSORS OF THE STATEMENT OF FIRST PRINCIPLES

ORGANIZATION	CONTACT	ADDRESS	TELEPHONE NUMBER	INTERNET WEBSITE
American Association of School Administrators	Dr. Paul Houston, Executive Director	1801 N. Moore St., Arlington, VA 22209	703-528-0700	n/a
American Center for Law and Justice	Jay Alan Sekulow, Chief Counsel	P.O. Box 64429, Virginia Beach, VA 23467	757-579-2489	www.aclj.org
American Center for Law and Justice, Office of Government Affairs	Colby May	1000 Thomas Jefferson St., N.W., Washington, D.C. 20007	202-337-2273	n/a
American Federation of Teachers	Sandra Feldman, President	555 New Jersey Ave., N.W., Washington, D.C. 20001	202-879-4400	www.aft.org
Anti-Defamation League	Abraham H. Foxman, Director	823 United Nations Plaza, New York, NY 10017	212-490-2525	www.adl.org
Anti-Defamation League	Michael Lieberman, Associate Director/ Legal Counsel	1100 Connecticut Ave., Suite 1020, Washington, D.C. 20036	202-452-8320	n/a
Association for Supervision and Curriculum Development	Gene Carter, Executive Director	1250 North Pitt St., Alexandria, VA 22314-1453	703-549-9110	www.ascd.org
Carnegie Foundation for the Advancement of Teaching	Dr. Lee S. Shulman, President	555 Middlefield Road, Menlo Park, CA 94025	650-849-8000	www.carnegiefoundation.org
Catholic League for Religious and Civil Rights	William A. Donohue, President	1011 First Ave., New York, NY 10022	703-538-5085	n/a
Central Conference of American Rabbis	Rabbi Richard Levy, President	355 Lexington Ave., New York, NY 10017	212-972-3636	www.ccarnet.org
Christian Coalition	Donald Hodel, President	1801 Sarah Drive, Suite L, Chesapeake, VA 23320	757-424-2630	www.cc.org

ORGANIZATION	CONTACT	ADDRESS	TELEPHONE NUMBER	INTERNET WEBSITE
Christian Educators Association International	Forrest Turpen, Executive Director	P.O. Box 41300, Pasadena, CA 91114-8300	818-798-1124	www.ceai.com
Christian Legal Society	Sam Casey, Executive Director	4208 Evergreen Lane, Suite 222, Annadale, VA 22003	703-642- 1070	www.cls.com
Citizens for Excellence in Education	Dr. Robert Simonds, President	P.O. Box 3200, Costa Mesa, CA 92628	949-251-9333	n/a
Council on Islamic Education	Shabbir Mansuri, Founding Director	P.O. Box 20186, Fountain Valley, CA 92728-0186	714-839-2929	n/a
First Amendment Center	Dr. Charles Haynes, Scholar in Residence	1207 18th Ave. S., Nashville, TN 37212	615-322- 9855	www.freedomforum.org/first/welcome.asp
National Association of Elementary School Principals	Samuel G. Sava, Executive Director	1615 Duke St., Alexandria, VA 22314-3483	703-684-3345	www.naesp.org
National Association of Evangelicals	The Rev. Dr. Don Argue, President	1023 15th St. N.W., Suite 500, Washington, D.C. 20005	202-789-1011	www.nae.net
National Association of Secondary School Principals	Timothy Dyer, Executive Director	1904 Association Drive, Reston, VA 20191-1537	703-860-0200	www.nassp.org
National Council of Churches	Joan B. Campbell, General Secretary	475 Riverside Drive, New York, NY 10115	212-870- 2227	n/a
National Education Association	Bob Chase, President	1201 16th St. N.W., Washington, D.C. 20036	202-833-4000	www.nea.org
National Parent Teacher Association	Lois Jean White, President	330 N. Wabash Ave., Suite 2100, Chicago, IL 60611-3690	312-670-678	www.pta.org
National School Boards Association	Anne Bryant, Executive Director	1680 Duke St., Alexandria, VA 22314	703-838-672	www.nsba.org
People for the American Way	Carol Shields, President	2000 M St. N.W., Suite 400, Washington, D.C. 20036	202-467-4999	n/a

APPENDIX 8

ORGANIZATION	CONTACT	ADDRESS	TELEPHONE NUMBER	INTERNET WEBSITE
Phi Delta Kappa	Ron Joekel, President	408 North Union St. P.O. Box 789, Bloomington, IN 47402-0789	800-766-1156	www.pdkintl.org
Union of American Hebrew Congregations	Rabbi David Saperstein, Director	2027 Massachusetts Ave. N.W., Washington, D.C. 20036	202-387-2800	n/a

APPENDIX 9:

THE EQUAL ACCESS ACT OF 1984 (20 U.S.C. 4071-74)

DENIAL OF EQUAL ACCESS PROHIBITED

Section 4071.

a. It shall be unlawful for any public secondary school which receives Federal financial assistance and which has a limited open forum to deny equal access or a fair opportunity to, or discriminate against, any students who wish to conduct a meeting within that limited open forum on the basis of the religious, political, philosophical, or other content of the speech at such meetings.

b. A public secondary school has a limited open forum whenever such school grants an offering to or opportunity for one or more noncurriculum-related student groups to meet on school premises during noninstructional time.

c. Schools shall be deemed to offer a fair opportunity to students who wish to conduct a meeting within its limited open forum if such school uniformly provides that—

1. the meeting is voluntary and student-initiated;

2. there is no sponsorship of the meeting by the school, the government, or its agents or employees;

3. employees or agents of the school or government are present at religious meetings only in a nonparticipatory capacity;

4. the meeting does not materially and substantially interfere with the orderly conduct of educational activities within the school; and

5. nonschool persons may not direct, conduct, control, or regularly attend activities of student groups.

d. Nothing in this subchapter shall be construed to authorize the United States or any State or political subdivision thereof —

1. to influence the form or content of any prayer or other religious activity;

2. to require any person to participate in prayer or other religious activity;

3. to expend public funds beyond the incidental cost of providing the space for student-initiated meetings;

4. to compel any school agent or employee to attend a school meeting if the content of the speech at the meeting is contrary to the beliefs of the agent or employee;

5. to sanction meetings that are otherwise unlawful;

6. to limit the rights of groups of students which are not of a specified numerical size; or

7. to abridge the constitutional rights of any person.

e. Notwithstanding the availability of any other remedy under the Constitution or the laws of the United States, nothing in this subchapter shall be construed to authorize the United States to deny or withhold Federal financial assistance to any school.

f. Nothing in this subchapter shall be construed to limit the authority of the school, its agents or employees, to maintain order and discipline on school premises, to protect the well- being of students and faculty, and to assure that attendance of students at meetings is voluntary.

DEFINITIONS

Section 4072. As used in this subchapter—

1. The term "secondary school" means a public school which provides secondary education as determined by State law.

2. The term "sponsorship" includes the act of promoting, leading, or participating in a meeting. The assignment of a teacher, administrator, or other school employee to a meeting for custodial purposes does not constitute sponsorship of the meeting.

3. The term "meeting" includes those activities of student groups which are permitted under a school's limited open forum and are not directly related to the school curriculum.

4. The term "noninstructional time" means time set aside by the school before actual classroom instruction begins or after actual classroom instruction ends.

SEVERABILITY

Section 4073.

If any provision of this subchapter or the application thereof to any person or circumstances is judicially determined to be invalid, the provisions of the remainder of the subchapter and the application to other persons or circumstances shall not be affected thereby.

CONSTRUCTION

Section 4074.

The provisions of this subchapter shall supersede all other provisions of Federal law that are inconsistent with the provisions of this subchapter.

APPENDIX 10:

AMERICAN INDIAN RELIGIOUS FREEDOM ACT OF 1978

SECTION 1996. Protection and Preservation of Traditional Religions of Native Americans.

On and after August 11, 1978, it shall be the policy of the United States to protect and preserve for American Indians their inherent right of freedom to believe, express, and exercise the traditional religions of the American Indian, Eskimo, Aleut, and Native Hawaiians, including but not limited to access to sites, use and possession of sacred objects, and the freedom to worship through ceremonials and traditional rites.

APPENDIX 11:

AMERICAN INDIAN RELIGIOUS FREEDOM ACT AMENDMENTS OF 1994 (PUBLIC LAW 103-344)

An Act to amend the American Indian Religious Freedom Act to provide for the traditional use of peyote by Indians for religious purposes, and for other purposes.

Be it enacted by the Senate and House of Representatives of the United States of America in Congress assembled,

SECTION 1. SHORT TITLE.

This Act may be cited as the "American Indian Religious Freedom Act Amendments of 1994".

SECTION 2. TRADITIONAL INDIAN RELIGIOUS USE OF THE PEYOTE SACRAMENT.

The Act of August 11, 1978 (42 U.S.C. 1996), commonly referred to as the "American Indian Religious Freedom Act", is amended by adding at the end thereof the following new section:

"SECTION 3. (a) The Congress finds and declares that—

"(1) for many Indian people, the traditional ceremonial use of the peyote cactus as a religious sacrament has for centuries been integral to a way of life, and significant in perpetuating Indian tribes and cultures;

"(2) since 1965, this ceremonial use of peyote by Indians has been protected by Federal regulation;

"(3) while at least 28 States have enacted laws which are similar to, or are in conformance with, the Federal regulation which protects the ceremonial use of peyote by Indian religious practitioners, 22 States have not done so, and this lack of uniformity has created hardship for Indian people who participate in such religious ceremonies;

"(4) the Supreme Court of the United States, in the case of Employment Division v. Smith, 494 U.S. 872 (1990), held that the First Amendment does not protect Indian practitioners who use peyote in Indian religious ceremonies, and also raised uncertainty whether this religious practice would be protected under the compelling State interest standard; and

"(5) the lack of adequate and clear legal protection for the religious use of peyote by Indians may serve to stigmatize and marginalize Indian tribes and cultures, and increase the risk that they will be exposed to discriminatory treatment.

"(b)(1) Notwithstanding any other provision of law, the use, possession, or transportation of peyote by an Indian for bona fide traditional ceremonial purposes in connection with the practice of a traditional Indian religion is lawful, and shall not be prohibited by the United States or any State. No Indian shall be penalized or discriminated against on the basis of such use, possession or transportation, including, but not limited to, denial of otherwise applicable benefits under public assistance programs.

"(b)(2) This section does not prohibit such reasonable regulation and registration by the Drug Enforcement Administration of those persons who cultivate, harvest, or distribute peyote as may be consistent with the purposes of this Act.

"(b)(3) This section does not prohibit application of the provisions of section 481.111(a) of Vernon's Texas Health and Safety Code Annotated, in effect on the date of enactment of this section, insofar as those provisions pertain to the cultivation, harvest, and distribution of peyote.

"(b)(4) Nothing in this section shall prohibit any Federal department or agency, in carrying out its statutory responsibilities and functions, from promulgating regulations establishing reasonable limitations on the use or ingestion of peyote prior to or during the performance of duties by sworn law enforcement officers or personnel directly involved in public transportation or any other safety-sensitive positions where the performance of such duties may be adversely affected by such use or ingestion. Such regulations shall be adopted only after consultation with representatives of traditional Indian religions for which the sacramental use of peyote is integral to their practice. Any regulation promulgated pursuant to this section shall be subject to the balancing test set forth in section 3 of the Religious Freedom Restoration Act (Public Law 103-141; 42 U.S.C. 2000bb-1).

"(b)(5) This section shall not be construed as requiring prison authorities to permit, nor shall it be construed to prohibit prison authorities from permitting, access to peyote by Indians while incarcerated within Federal or State prison facilities.

"(b)(6) Subject to the provisions of the Religious Freedom Restoration Act (Public Law 103-141; 42 U.S.C. 2000bb-1), this section shall not be construed to prohibit States from enacting or enforcing reasonable traffic safety laws or regulations.

"(b)(7) Subject to the provisions of the Religious Freedom Restoration Act (Public Law 103-141; 42 USC 2000bb-1), this section does not prohibit the Secretary of Defense from promulgating regulations establishing reasonable limitations on the use, possession, transportation, or distribution of peyote to promote military readiness, safety, or compliance with international law or laws of other countries. Such regulations shall be adopted only after consultation with representatives of traditional Indian religions for which the sacramental use of peyote is integral to their practice.

"(c) For purposes of this section—

"(1) the term 'Indian' means a member of an Indian tribe;

"(2) the term 'Indian tribe' means any tribe, band, nation, pueblo, or other organized group or community of Indians, including any Alaska Native village (as defined in, or established pursuant to, the Alaska Native Claims Settlement Act (43 U.S.C. 1601 et seq.)), which is recognized as eligible for the special programs and services provide by the United States to Indians because of their status as Indians;

"(3) the term 'Indian religion' means any religion—

"(A) which is practiced by Indians; and

"(B) the origin and interpretation of which is from within a traditional Indian culture or community; and

"(4) the term 'State' means any State of the United States and any political subdivision thereof.

"(d) Nothing in this section shall be construed as abrogating, diminishing, or otherwise affecting—

"(1) the inherent rights of any Indian tribe;

"(2) the rights, express or implicit, of any Indian tribe which exist under treaties, Executive orders, and laws of the United States;

"(3) the inherent right of Indians to practice their religions; and

"(4) the right of Indians to practice their religions under any Federal or State law.".

APPENDIX 12:

THE WILLIAMSBURG CHARTER

PRELIMINARY STATEMENT

Keenly aware of the high national purpose of commemorating the bicentennial of the United States Constitution, we who sign this Charter seek to celebrate the Constitution's greatness, and to call for a bold reaffirmation and reappraisal of its vision and guiding principles. In particular, we call for a fresh consideration of religious liberty in our time, and of the place of the First Amendment Religious Liberty clauses in our national life.

We gratefully acknowledge that the Constitution has been hailed as America's "chief export" and "the most wonderful work ever struck off at a given time by the brain and purpose of man." Today, two hundred years after its signing, the Constitution is not only the world's oldest, still-effective written constitution, but the admired pattern of ordered liberty for countless people in many lands.

In spite of its enduring and universal qualities, however, some provisions of the Constitution are now the subject of widespread controversy in the United States. One area of intense controversy concerns the First Amendment Religious Liberty clauses, whose mutually reinforcing provisions act as a double guarantee of religious liberty, one part barring the making of any law "respecting an establishment of religion" and the other barring any law "prohibiting the free exercise thereof."

The First Amendment Religious Liberty provisions epitomize the Constitution's visionary realism. They were, as James Madison said, the "true remedy" to the predicament of religious conflict they originally addressed, and they well express the responsibilities and limits of the state with respect to liberty and justice.

Our commemoration of the Constitution's bicentennial must therefore go beyond celebration to rededication. Unless this is done, an irreplaceable part of national life will be endangered, and a remarkable opportunity for the expansion of liberty will be lost. For we judge that the present controversies over religion in public life pose both a danger and an opportunity. There is evident danger in the fact that certain forms of politically reassertive religion in parts of the world are, in principle, enemies of democratic freedom and a source of deep social antagonism. There is also evident opportunity in the growing philosophical and cultural awareness that all people live by commitments and ideals, that value-neutrality is impossible in the ordering of society, and that we are on the edge of a promising moment for a fresh assessment of pluralism and liberty. It is with an eye to both the promise and the peril that we publish this Charter and pledge ourselves to its principles.

We readily acknowledge our continuing differences. Signing this Charter implies no pretense that we believe the same things or that our differences over policy proposals, legal interpretations and philosophical groundings do not ultimately matter. The truth is not even that what unites us is deeper than what divides us, for differences over belief are the deepest and least easily negotiated of all.

The Charter sets forth a renewed national compact, in the sense of a solemn mutual agreement between parties, on how we view the place of religion in American life and how we should contend with each other's deepest differences in the public sphere. It is a call to a vision of public life that will allow conflict to lead to consensus, religious commitment to reinforce political civility. In this way, diversity is not a point of weakness but a source of strength.

I. A TIME FOR REAFFIRMATION

We believe, in the first place, that the nature of the Religious Liberty clauses must be understood before the problems surrounding them can be resolved. We therefore affirm both their cardinal assumptions and the reasons for their crucial national importance.

With regard to the assumptions of the First Amendment Religious Liberty clauses, we hold three to be chief:

1. The Inalienable Right

Nothing is more characteristic of humankind than the natural and inescapable drive toward meaning and belonging, toward making sense of life and finding community in the world. As fundamental and precious as life itself, this "will to meaning" finds expression in ultimate beliefs, whether theistic or non-theistic, transcendent or naturalistic, and these beliefs are most our own when a matter of conviction rather than coercion. They are most our own when, in the words of George Mason, the principal author of the Virginia Declaration of Rights, they are "directed only by reason and conviction, not by force or violence."

As James Madison expressed it in his Memorial and Remonstrance, "The Religion then of every man must be left to the conviction and conscience of every man; and it is the right of every man to exercise it as these may dictate. This right is in its nature an unalienable right."

Two hundred years later, despite dramatic changes in life and a marked increase of naturalistic philosophies in some parts of the world and in certain sectors of our society, this right to religious liberty based upon freedom of conscience remains fundamental and inalienable. While particular beliefs may be true or false, better or worse, the right to reach, hold, exercise them freely, or change them, is basic and non-negotiable.

Religious liberty finally depends on neither the favors of the state and its officials nor the vagaries of tyrants or majorities. Religious liberty in a democracy is a right that may not be submitted to vote and depends on the outcome of no election. A society is only as just and free as it is respectful of this right, especially toward the beliefs of its smallest minorities and least popular communities.

The right to freedom of conscience is premised not upon science, nor upon social utility, nor upon pride of species. Rather, it is premised upon the inviolable dignity of the human person. It is the foundation of, and is integrally related to, all other rights and freedoms secured by the Constitution. This basic civil liberty is clearly acknowledged in the Declaration of Independence and is ineradicable from the long tradition of rights and liberties from which the Revolution sprang.

2. The Ever Present Danger

No threat to freedom of conscience and religious liberty has historically been greater than the coercions of both Church and State. These two institutions—the one religious, the other political—have through the centuries succumbed to the temptation of coercion in their claims over minds and souls. When these institutions and their claims have been combined, it has too often resulted in terrible violations of human liberty and dignity. They are so combined when the sword and purse of the State are in the hands of the Church, or when the State usurps the mantle of the Church so as to coerce the conscience and compel belief. These and other such confusions of religion and state authority represent the misordering of religion and government which it is the purpose of the Religious Liberty provisions to prevent.

Authorities and orthodoxies have changed, kingdoms and empires have come and gone, yet as John Milton once warned, "new Presbyter is but old priest writ large." Similarly, the modern persecutor of religion is but ancient tyrant with more refined instruments of control. Moreover, many of the greatest crimes against conscience of this century have been committed, not by religious authorities, but by ideologues virulently opposed to traditional religion.

Yet whether ancient or modern, issuing from religion or ideology, the result is the same: religious and ideological orthodoxies, when politically established, lead only too naturally toward what Roger Williams called a "spiritual rape" that coerces the conscience and produces "rivers of civil blood" that stain the record of human history.

Less dramatic but also lethal to freedom and the chief menace to religious liberty today is the expanding power of government control over personal behavior and the institutions of society, when the government acts not so much in deliberate hostility to, but in reckless disregard of, communal belief and personal conscience.

Thanks principally to the wisdom of the First Amendment, the American experience is different. But even in America where state-established orthodoxies are unlawful and the state is constitutionally limited, religious liberty can never be taken for granted. It is a rare achievement that requires constant protection.

3. The Most Nearly Perfect Solution

Knowing well that "nothing human can be perfect" (James Madison) and that the Constitution was not "a faultless work" (Gouverneur Morris), the Framers nevertheless saw the First Amendment as a "true remedy" and the most nearly perfect solution yet devised for properly ordering the relationship of religion and the state in a free society.

There have been occasions when the protections of the First Amendment have been overridden or imperfectly applied. Nonetheless, the First Amendment is a momentous decision for religious liberty, the most important political decision for religious liberty and public justice in the history of humankind. Limitation upon religious liberty is allowable only where the State has borne a heavy burden of proof that the limitation is justified—not by any ordinary public interest, but by a supreme public necessity—and that no less restrictive alternative to limitation exists.

The Religious Liberty clauses are a brilliant construct in which both No establishment and Free exercise serve the ends of religious liberty and freedom of conscience. No longer can sword, purse and sacred mantle be equated. Now, the government is barred from using religion's mantle to become a confessional State, and from allowing religion to use the government's sword and purse to become a coercing Church. In this new order, the freedom of the government from religious control and the freedom of religion from government control are a double guarantee of the protection of rights. No faith is preferred or prohibited, for where there is no state-definable orthodoxy, there can be no state-punishable heresy.

With regard to the reasons why the First Amendment Religious Liberty clauses are important for the nation today, we hold five to be pre-eminent:

1. The First Amendment Religious Liberty provisions have both a logical and historical priority in the Bill of Rights. They have logical priority because the security of all rights rests upon the recognition that they are neither given by the state, nor can they be taken away by the state. Such rights are inherent in the inviolability of the human person. History demonstrates that unless these rights are protected our society's slow, painful progress toward freedom would not have been possible.

2. The First Amendment Religious Liberty provisions lie close to the heart of the distinctiveness of the American experiment. The uniqueness of the American way of disestablishment and its consequences have often been more obvious to foreign observers such as Alexis de Tocqueville and Lord James Bryce, who wrote that "of all the differences between the Old world and the New, this is perhaps the most salient." In particular, the Religious Liberty clauses are vital to harnessing otherwise centrifugal forces such as personal liberty and social diversity, thus sustaining republican vitality while making possible a necessary measure of national concord.

3. The First Amendment Religious Liberty provisions are the democratic world's most salient alternative to the totalitarian repression of human rights and provide a corrective to unbridled nationalism and religious warfare around the world.

4. The First Amendment Religious Liberty provisions provide the United States' most distinctive answer to one of the world's most pressing questions in the late-twentieth century. They address the problem: How do we live with each other's deepest differences? How do religious convictions and political freedom complement rather than threaten each other on a small planet in a pluralistic age? In a world in which bigotry, fanaticism, terrorism and the state control of religion are all too common responses to these questions, sustaining the justice and liberty of the American arrangement is an urgent moral task.

5. The First Amendment Religious Liberty provisions give American society a unique position in relation to both the First and Third worlds. Highly modernized like the rest of the First World, yet not so secularized, this society—largely because of religious freedom—remains, like most of the Third World, deeply religious. This fact, which is critical for

possibilities of better human understanding, has not been sufficiently appreciated in American self-understanding, or drawn upon in American diplomacy and communication throughout the world.

In sum, as much if not more than any other single provision in the entire Constitution, the Religious Liberty provisions hold the key to American distinctiveness and American destiny. Far from being settled by the interpretations of judges and historians, the last word on the First Amendment likely rests in a chapter yet to be written, documenting the unfolding drama of America. If religious liberty is neglected, all civil liberties will suffer. If it is guarded and sustained, the American experiment will be the more secure.

II. A TIME FOR REAPPRAISAL

Much of the current controversy about religion and politics neither reflects the highest wisdom of the First Amendment nor serves the best interests of the disputants or the nation. We therefore call for a critical reappraisal of the course and consequences of such controversy. Four widespread errors have exacerbated the controversy needlessly.

1. The Issue Is Not Only What We Debate, But How

The debate about religion in public life is too often misconstrued as a clash of ideologies alone, pitting "secularists" against the "sectarians" or vice versa. Though competing and even contrary worldviews are involved, the controversy is not solely ideological. It also flows from a breakdown in understanding of how personal and communal beliefs should be related to public life.

The American republic depends upon the answers to two questions. By what ultimate truths ought we to live? And how should these be related to public life? The first question is personal, but has a public dimension because of the connection between beliefs and public virtue. The American answer to the first question is that the government is excluded from giving an answer. The second question, however, is thoroughly public in character, and a public answer is appropriate and necessary to the well-being of this society.

This second question was central to the idea of the First Amendment. The Religious Liberty provisions are not "articles of faith" concerned with the substance of particular doctrines or of policy issues. They are "articles of peace" concerned with the constitutional constraints and the shared prior understanding within which the American people can engage their differences in a civil manner and thus provide for both religious liberty and stable public government.

Conflicts over the relationship between deeply held beliefs and public policy will remain a continuing feature of democratic life. They do not discredit the First Amendment, but confirm its wisdom and point to the need to distinguish the Religious Liberty clauses from the particular controversies they address. The clauses can never be divorced from the controversies they address, but should always be held distinct. In the public discussion, an open commitment to the constraints and standards of the clauses should precede and accompany debate over the controversies.

2. The Issue Is Not Sectarian, But National

The role of religion in American public life is too often devalued or dismissed in public debate, as though the American people's historically vital religious traditions were at best a purely private matter and at worst essentially sectarian and divisive.

Such a position betrays a failure of civil respect for the convictions of others. It also underestimates the degree to which the Framers relied on the American people's religious convictions to be what Tocqueville described as "the first of their political institutions." In America, this crucial public role has been played by diverse beliefs, not so much despite disestablishment as because of disestablishment.

The Founders knew well that the republic they established represented an audacious gamble against long historical odds. This form of government depends upon ultimate beliefs, for otherwise we have no right to the rights by which it thrives, yet rejects any official formulation of them. The republic will therefore always remain an "undecided experiment" that stands or falls by the dynamism of its non- established faiths.

3. The Issue Is Larger Than the Disputants

Recent controversies over religion and public life have too often become a form of warfare in which individuals, motives and reputations have been impugned. The intensity of the debate is commensurate with the importance of the issues debated, but to those engaged in this warfare we present two arguments for reappraisal and restraint.

The lesser argument is one of expediency and is based on the ironic fact that each side has become the best argument for the other. One side's excesses have become the other side's arguments; one side's extremists the other side's recruiters. The danger is that, as the ideological warfare becomes self-perpetuating, more serious issues and broader national interests will be forgotten and the bitterness deepened.

The more important argument is one of principle and is based on the fact that the several sides have pursued their objectives in ways which contradict their own best ideals. Too often, for example, religious believers have been uncharitable, liberals have been illiberal, conservatives have been insensitive to tradition, champions of tolerance have been intolerant, defenders of free speech have been censorious, and citizens of a republic based on democratic accommodation have succumbed to a habit of relentless confrontation.

4. The Issue Is Understandably Threatening

The First Amendment's meaning is too often debated in ways that ignore the genuine grievances or justifiable fears of opposing points of view. This happens when the logic of opposing arguments favors either an unwarranted intrusion of religion into public life or an unwarranted exclusion of religion from it. History plainly shows that with religious control over government, political freedom dies; with political control over religion, religious freedom dies.

The First Amendment has contributed to avoiding both these perils, but this happy experience is no cause for complacency. Though the United States has escaped the worst excesses experienced elsewhere in the world, the republic has shown two distinct tendencies of its own, one in the past and one today.

In earlier times, though lasting well into the twentieth century, there was a de facto semi-establishment of one religion in the United States: a generalized Protestantism given dominant status in national institutions, especially in the public schools. This development was largely approved by Protestants, but widely opposed by non-Protestants, including Catholics and Jews.

In more recent times, and partly in reaction, constitutional jurisprudence has tended, in the view of many, to move toward the *de facto* semi-establishment of a wholly secular understanding of the origin, nature and destiny of humankind and of the American nation. During this period, the exclusion of teaching about the role of religion in society, based partly upon a misunderstanding of First Amendment decisions, has ironically resulted in giving a dominant status to such wholly secular understandings in many national institutions. Many secularists appear as unconcerned over the consequences of this development as were Protestants unconcerned about their *de facto* establishment earlier.

Such de facto establishments, though seldom extreme, usually benign and often unwitting, are the source of grievances and fears among the several parties in current controversies. Together with the encroachments of the expanding modern state, such *de facto* establishments, as much as any official establishment, are likely to remain a threat to freedom and justice for all.

Justifiable fears are raised by those who advocate theocracy or the coercive power of law to establish a "Christian America." While this advocacy is and should be legally protected, such proposals contradict freedom of conscience and the genius of the Religious Liberty provisions.

At the same time there are others who raise justifiable fears of an unwarranted exclusion of religion from public life. The assertion of moral judgments as though they were morally neutral, and interpretations of the "wall of separation" that would exclude religious expression and argument from public life, also contradict freedom of conscience and the genius of the provisions.

Civility obliges citizens in a pluralistic society to take great care in using words and casting issues. The communications media have a primary role, and thus a special responsibility, in shaping public opinion and debate. Words such as public, secular and religious should be free from discriminatory bias. "Secular purpose," for example, should not mean "non-religious purpose" but "general public purpose." Otherwise, the impression is gained that "public is equivalent to secular; religion is equivalent to private." Such equations are neither accurate nor just.

Similarly, it is false to equate "public" and "governmental." In a society that sets store by the necessary limits on government, there are many spheres of life that are public but non-governmental.

Two important conclusions follow from a reappraisal of the present controversies over religion in public life. First, the process of adjustment and readjustment to the constraints and standards of the Religious Liberty provisions is an ongoing requirement of American democracy. The Constitution is not a self-interpreting, self-executing document; and the prescriptions of the Religious Liberty provisions cannot by themselves resolve the myriad confusions and ambiguities surrounding the right ordering of the relationship between religion and government in a free society. The Framers clearly understood that the Religious Liberty provisions provide the legal construct for what must be an ongoing process of adjustment and mutual give-and-take in a democracy.

We are keenly aware that, especially over state- supported education, we as a people must continue to wrestle with the complex connections between religion and the transmission of moral values in a pluralistic society. Thus, we cannot have, and should not seek, a definitive, once for all solution to the questions that will continue to surround the Religious Liberty provisions.

Second, the need for such a readjustment today can best be addressed by remembering that the two clauses are essentially one provision for preserving religious liberty. Both parts, No establishment and Free exercise, are to be comprehensively understood as being in the service of religious liberty as a positive good. At the heart of the Establishment clause is the prohibition of state sponsorship of religion and at the heart of Free Exercise clause is the prohibition of state interference with religious liberty.

No sponsorship means that the state must leave to the free citizenry the public expression of ultimate beliefs, religious or otherwise, providing only that no expression is excluded from, and none governmentally favored, in the continuing democratic discourse.

No interference means the assurance of voluntary religious expression free from governmental intervention. This includes placing religious expression on an equal footing with all other forms of expression in genuinely public forums.

No sponsorship and no interference together mean fair opportunity. That is to say, all faiths are free to enter vigorously into public life and to exercise such influence as their followers and ideas engender. Such democratic exercise of influence is in the best tradition of American voluntarism and is not an unwarranted "imposition" or "establishment."

III. A TIME FOR RECONSTITUTION

We believe, finally, that the time is ripe for a genuine expansion of democratic liberty, and that this goal may be attained through a new engagement of citizens in a debate that is reordered in accord with constitutional first principles and considerations of the common good. This amounts to no less than the reconstitution of a free republican people in our day. Careful consideration of three precepts would advance this possibility:

1. The Criteria Must Be Multiple

Reconstitution requires the recognition that the great dangers in interpreting the Constitution today are either to release interpretation from any demanding criteria or to narrow the criteria excessively. The first relaxes the necessary restraining force of the Constitution, while the second overlooks the insights that have arisen from the Constitution in two centuries of national experience.

Religious liberty is the only freedom in the First Amendment to be given two provisions. Together the clauses form a strong bulwark against suppression of religious liberty, yet they emerge from a series of dynamic tensions which cannot ultimately be relaxed. The Religious Liberty provisions grow out of an understanding not only of rights and a due recognition of faiths but of realism and a due recognition of factions. They themselves reflect both faith and skepticism. They raise questions of equality and liberty, majority rule and minority rights, individual convictions and communal tradition.

The Religious Liberty provisions must be understood both in terms of the Framers' intentions and history's sometimes surprising results. Interpreting and applying them today requires not only historical research but moral and political reflection.

The intention of the Framers is therefore a necessary but insufficient criterion for interpreting and applying the Constitution. But applied by itself, without any consideration of immutable principles of justice, the intention can easily be wielded as a weapon for governmental or sectarian causes, some quoting Jefferson and brandishing No establishment and others citing Madison and brandishing Free exercise. Rather, we must take the purpose and text of the Constitution seriously, sustain the principles behind the words and add an appreciation of the many-sided genius of the First Amendment and its complex development over time.

2. The Consensus Must Be Dynamic

Reconstitution requires a shared understanding of the relationship between the Constitution and the society it is to serve. The Framers understood that the Constitution is more than parchment and ink. The principles embodied in the document must be affirmed in practice by a free people since these principles reflect everything that constitutes the essential forms and substance of their society—the institutions, customs and ideals as well as the laws. Civic vitality and the effectiveness of law can be undermined when they overlook this broader cultural context of the Constitution.

Notable, in this connection is the striking absence today of any national consensus about religious liberty as a positive good. Yet religious liberty is indisputably what the Framers intended and what the First Amendment has preserved. Far from being a matter of exemption, exception or even toleration, religious liberty is an inalienable right. Far from being a sub-category of free speech or a constitutional redundancy, religious liberty is distinct and foundational. Far from being simply an individual right, religious liberty is a positive social good. Far from denigrating religion as a social or political "problem," the separation of Church and State is both the saving of religion from the temptation of political power and an achievement inspired in large part by religion itself. Far from weakening religion, disestablishment has, as an historical fact, enabled it to flourish.

In light of the First Amendment, the government should stand in relation to the churches, synagogues and other communities of faith as the guarantor of freedom. In light of the First Amendment, the churches, synagogues and other communities of faith stand in relation to the government as generators of faith, and therefore contribute to the spiritual and moral foundations of democracy. Thus, the government acts as a safeguard, but not the source, of freedom for faiths, whereas the churches and synagogues act as a source, but not the safeguard, of faiths for freedom.

The Religious Liberty provisions work for each other and for the federal idea as a whole. Neither established nor excluded, neither preferred nor proscribed, each faith (whether transcendent or naturalistic) is brought into a relationship with the government so that each is separated from the state in terms of its institutions, but democratically related to the state in terms of individuals and its ideas.

The result is neither a naked public square where all religion is excluded, nor a sacred public square with any religion established or semi-established. The result, rather, is a civil public square in which citizens of all religious faiths, or none, engage one another in the continuing democratic discourse.

3. The Compact Must Be Mutual

Reconstitution of a free republican people requires the recognition that religious liberty is a universal right joined to a universal duty to respect that right.

In the turns and twists of history, victims of religious discrimination have often later become perpetrators. In the famous image of Roger Williams, those at the helm of the Ship of State forget they were once under the hatches. They have, he said, "One weight for themselves when they are under the hatches, and another for others when they come to the helm." They show themselves, said James Madison, "as ready to set up an establishment which is to take them in as they were to pull down that which shut them out." Thus, benignly or otherwise, Protestants have treated Catholics as they were once treated, and secularists have done likewise with both.

Such inconsistencies are the natural seedbed for the growth of a de facto establishment. Against such inconsistencies we affirm that a right for one is a right for another and a responsibility for all. A right for a Protestant is a right for an Orthodox is a right for a Catholic is a right for a Jew is a right for a Humanist is a right for a Mormon is a right for a Muslim is a right for a Buddhist—and for the followers of any other faith within the wide bounds of the republic.

That rights are universal and responsibilities mutual is both the premise and the promise of democratic pluralism. The First Amendment, in this sense, is the epitome of public justice and serves as the Golden Rule for civic life. Rights are best guarded and responsibilities best exercised when each person and group guards for all others those rights they wish guarded for themselves. Whereas the wearer of the English crown is officially the Defender of the Faith, all who uphold the American Constitution are defenders of the rights of all faiths.

From this axiom, that rights are universal and responsibilities mutual, derives guidelines for conducting public debates involving religion in a manner that is democratic and civil. These guidelines are not, and must not be, mandated by law. But they are, we believe, necessary to reconstitute and revitalize the American understanding of the role of religion in a free society.

First, those who claim the right to dissent should assume the responsibility to debate: Commitment to democratic pluralism assumes the coexistence within one political community of groups whose ultimate faith commitments may be incompatible, yet whose common commitment to social unity and diversity does justice to both the requirements of individual conscience and the wider community. A general consent to the obligations of citizenship is therefore inherent in the American experiment, both as a founding principle ("We the people") and as a matter of daily practice.

There must always be room for those who do not wish to participate in the public ordering of our common life, who desire to pursue their own religious witness separately as conscience dictates. But at the same time, for those who do wish to participate, it should be understood that those claiming the right to dissent should assume the responsibility to debate. As this responsibility is exercised, the characteristic American formula of individual liberty complemented by respect for the opinions of others permits differences to be asserted, yet a broad, active community of understanding to be sustained.

Second, those who claim the right to criticize should assume the responsibility to comprehend: One of the ironies of democratic life is that freedom of conscience is jeopardized by false tolerance as well as by outright intolerance. Genuine tolerance considers contrary views fairly and judges them on merit. Debased tolerance so refrains from making any judgment that it refuses to listen at all. Genuine tolerance honestly weighs honest differences and promotes both impartiality and pluralism. Debased tolerance results in indifference to the differences that vitalize a pluralistic democracy.

Central to the difference between genuine and debased tolerance is the recognition that peace and truth must be held in tension. Pluralism must not be confused with, and is in fact endangered by, philosophical and ethical indifference. Commitment to strong, clear philosophical and ethical ideas need not imply either intolerance or opposition to democratic pluralism. On the contrary, democratic pluralism requires an agreement to be locked in public argument over disagreements of consequence within the bonds of civility.

The right to argue for any public policy is a fundamental right for every citizen; respecting that right is a fundamental responsibility for all other citizens. When any view is expressed, all must uphold as constitutionally protected its advocate's right to express it. But others are free to challenge that view as politically pernicious, philosophically false, ethically evil, theologically idolatrous, or simply absurd, as the case may be seen to be.

Unless this tension between peace and truth is respected, civility cannot be sustained. In that event, tolerance degenerates into either apathetic relativism or a dogmatism as uncritical of itself as it is uncomprehending of others. The result is a general corruption of principled public debate.

Third, those who claim the right to influence should accept the responsibility not to inflame: Too often in recent disputes over religion and public affairs, some have insisted that any evidence of religious influence on public policy represents an establishment of religion and is therefore precluded as an improper "imposition." Such exclusion of religion from public life is historically unwarranted, philosophically inconsistent and profoundly undemocratic. The Framers' intention is indisputably ignored when public policy debates can appeal to the theses of Adam Smith and Karl Marx, or Charles Darwin and Sigmund Freud but not to the Western religious tradition in general and the Hebrew and Christian Scriptures in particular. Many of the most dynamic social movements in American history, including that of civil rights, were legitimately inspired and shaped by religious motivation.

Freedom of conscience and the right to influence public policy on the basis of religiously informed ideas are inseverably linked. In short, a key to democratic renewal is the fullest possible participation in the most open possible debate.

Religious liberty and democratic civility are also threatened, however, from another quarter. Overreacting to an improper veto on religion in public life, many have used religious language and images not for the legitimate influencing of policies but to inflame politics. Politics is indeed an extension of ethics and therefore engages religious principles; but some err by refusing to recognize that there is a distinction, though not a separation, between religion and politics. As a result, they bring to politics a misplaced absoluteness that idolizes politics, "Satanizes" their enemies and politicizes their own faith.

Even the most morally informed policy positions involve prudential judgments as well as pure principle. Therefore, to make an absolute equation of principles and policies inflates politics and does violence to reason, civil life and faith itself. Politics has recently been inflamed by a number of confusions: the confusion of personal religious affiliation with qualification or disqualification for public office; the confusion of claims to divine guidance with claims to divine endorsement; and the confusion of government neutrality among faiths with government indifference or hostility to religion.

Fourth, those who claim the right to participate should accept the responsibility to persuade: Central to the American experience is the power of political persuasion. Growing partly from principle and partly from the pressures of democratic pluralism, commitment to persuasion is the corollary of the belief that conscience is inviolable, coercion of conscience is evil, and the public interest is best served by consent hard won from vigorous debate. Those who believe themselves privy to the will of history brook no argument and need never tarry for consent. But to those who subscribe to the idea of government by the consent of the governed, compelled beliefs are a violation of first principles. The natural logic of the Religious Liberty provisions is to foster a political culture of persuasion which admits the challenge of opinions from all sources.

Arguments for public policy should be more than private convictions shouted out loud. For persuasion to be principled, private convictions should be translated into publicly accessible claims. Such public claims should be made publicly accessible for two reasons: first, because they must engage those who do not share the same private convictions, and second, because they should be directed toward the common good.

RENEWAL OF FIRST PRINCIPLES

We who live in the third century of the American republic can learn well from the past as we look to the future. Our Founders were both idealists and realists. Their confidence in human abilities was tempered by their skepticism about human nature. Aware of what was new in their times, they also knew the need for renewal in times after theirs. "No free government, or the blessings of liberty," wrote George Mason in 1776, "can be preserved to any people, but by a firm adherence to justice, moderation, temperance, frugality, and virtue, and by frequent recurrence to fundamental principles."

True to the ideals and realism of that vision, we who sign this Charter, people of many and various beliefs, pledge ourselves to the enduring precepts of the First Amendment as the cornerstone of the American experiment in liberty under law.

We address ourselves to our fellow citizens, daring to hope that the strongest desire of the greatest number is for the common good. We are firmly persuaded that the principles asserted here require a fresh consideration, and that the renewal of religious liberty is crucial to sustain a free people that would remain free. We therefore commit ourselves to speak, write and act according to this vision and these principles. We urge our fellow citizens to do the same.

To agree on such guiding principles and to achieve such a compact will not be easy. Whereas a law is a command directed to us, a compact is a promise that must proceed freely from us. To achieve it demands a measure of the vision, sacrifice and perseverance shown by our Founders. Their task was to defy the past, seeing and securing religious liberty against the terrible precedents of history. Ours is to challenge the future, sustaining vigilance and broadening protections against every new menace, including that of our own complacency. Knowing the unquenchable desire for freedom, they lit a beacon. It is for us who know its blessings to keep it burning brightly.

GLOSSARY

GLOSSARY

Abolish - To repeal or revoke, such as a law or custom.

Action at Law - A judicial proceeding whereby one party prosecutes another for a wrong done.

Actionable - Giving rise to a cause of action.

American Civil Liberties Union (ACLU) - A nationwide organization dedicated to the enforcement and preservation of rights and civil liberties guaranteed by the federal and state constitutions.

Appeal - Resort to a higher court for the purpose of obtaining a review of a lower court decision.

Appellate Court - A court having jurisdiction to review the law as applied to a prior determination of the same case. proceeding.

Bigamy - The criminal offense of willfully and knowingly contracting a second marriage while the first marriage is still undissolved.

Bill of Rights - The first eight amendments to the United States Constitution.

Breach of Duty - In a general sense, any violation or omission of a legal or moral duty.

Capacity - Capacity is the legal qualification concerning the ability of one to understand the nature and effects of one's acts.

Charity - For income tax purposes, a charity is a nonprofit institution organized and operated exclusively for charitable purposes, whose income is exempt from federal income tax.

Child Abuse - Any form of cruelty to a child's physical, moral or mental well-being.

Child Custody - The care, control and maintenance of a child which may be awarded by a court to one of the parents of the child.

Child Welfare - A generic term which embraces the totality of measures necessary for a child's well being; physical, moral and mental.

Circuit Court - One of several courts in a given jurisdiction.

Civil Rights Act of 1964 - The federal act passed to provide stronger protection for rights guaranteed by the Constitution, such as voting rights.

Common Law - Common law is the system of jurisprudence which originated in England and was later applied in the United States.

Conscientious Objector - One who because of religious belief is opposed to any form of participation in a war.

Constitution - The fundamental principles of law which frame a governmental system.

Constitutional Right - Refers to the individual liberties granted by the constitution of a state or the federal government.

Court - The branch of government responsible for the resolution of disputes arising under the laws of the government.

Ecclesiastical Law - The body of jurisprudence administered by the ecclesiastical courts of England derived from the canon and civil law.

Parens Patriae - Latin for "parent of his country." Refers to the role of the state as guardian of legally disabled individuals.

Prisoner - One who is confined to a prison or other penal institution for the purpose of awaiting trial for a crime, or serving a sentence after conviction of a crime.

Rational Basis Test - The constitutional analysis of a law to determine whether it has a reasonable relationship to some legitimate government objective so as to uphold the law.

Remedy - Refers to the means by which a right is enforced or a violation of a right is compensated.

Separation of Power - The doctrine which prohibits one branch of the government from exercising the powers belonging to another branch of government.

Standing - The legal right of an individual or group to use the courts to resolve an existing controversy.

Supreme Court - In most jurisdictions, the Supreme Court is the highest appellate court, including the federal court system.

Trial Court - The court of original jurisdiction over a particular matter.

Unconstitutional - Refers to a statute which conflicts with the United States Constitution rendering it void.

Ward - A person over whom a guardian is appointed to manage his or her affairs.

Zoning - The government regulation of land use.

BIBLIOGRAPHY

BIBLIOGRAPHY

The American Civil Liberties Union. (Date Visited: September 1998) http:www.aclu.org.

Black's Law Dictionary, Fifth Edition. St. Paul, MN: West Publishing Company, 1979.

Cornell Law School Legal Information Institute. (Date Visited: September 1998) http://www.law.cornell.edu/.

The First Amendment Center. (Date Visited: September 1998) http://www.freedomforum.org/first/welcome.asp/.

Flowers, Ronald B. *That Godless Court: Supreme Court Decisions on Church-State Relationships.* Louisville, KY: Westminster John Knox Press, 1994.

Lynn, Barry, Stern, Marc D., and Thomas, Oliver S. *The Right to Religious Liberty*. New York, NY: The American Civil Liberties Union, 1995.

The United States Department of Education (Date Visited: September 1998) http://www.ed.gov/.